Beginning English Writing Skills

A Handbook with Practice

Mona Scheraga

National Textbook Company
a division of NTC/CONTEMPORARY PUBLISHING GROUP
Lincolnwood, Illinois USA

To my mother and father,

Jean and Ben Liechenstein,

whose faith and encouragement have made it all possible.

Publisher: Steve VanThournout

Editorial Director: Cindy Krejcsi

Executive Editor: Mary Jane Maples

Editor: Paula Eacott

Art Director: Ophelia M. Chambliss

Cover design: Ellen Pettengell

Interior design: Lynne Grenier

Production Manager: Margo Goia

Production Coordinator: Denise Duffy

ISBN: 0-8442-0475-7

Acknowledgments begin on page iv, which is to be considered an extension of this copyright page.

Published by National Textbook Company,
a division of NTC/Contemporary Publishing Group, Inc.

Beginning English Writing Skills

Contents

iv

Acknowledgments

Working with Becky Rauff, my editor on the original project, with Mary Jane Maples, my revision editor and purveyor of great ideas and humor, and with editor Paula Eacott of the intimidating credentials has been a special privilege. Their patience, insight, and expertise cannot be overestimated. The thousands of students who passed through my classes in more than twenty-five years of teaching deserve a special thanks. Each, in turn, helped fine-tune my understanding of the infinite dimensions of the teaching/learning process. To my husband, Murray, for being confidant and critic, artist and proofreader, and chief cook and pot scrubber during the revising of this text, go the thanks of an extremely grateful if sometimes neglectful wife.

I really must thank the profession, teachers of English to speakers of other languages, for the friends I've made in the field. For their advice and support go thanks to Penny Cameron, Sandy Briggs, Alison Rice, and Connie Attanasio, who can always be counted on, and to the many teachers in the Clark County Las Vegas school district and New York, in particular, whose suggestions have inspired the additions and the division of *Practical English Writing Skills* into two books.

I am grateful to the Fair Lawn Library, Fair Lawn, New Jersey, for use of its library card application and to Beverly Witwer of Iowa City, Iowa, for carrying the *Iowa Driver's Manual* all the way to Belarus. I also appreciate the gracious help of Valerie Schroder, chemistry teacher, and Alfred Brown, chair of the Science Department, at Passaic High School, Passaic, New Jersey. The English teachers of Belarus were a special inspiration.

I would like to acknowledge all the people I have worked with and learned from over the years. I am not unaware of how lucky I am to have been exposed to so many meaningful experiences in and out of the classroom.

Introduction

*B*eginning English Writing Skills is a guide to developing the writing skills we all need to function and succeed in our everyday lives—at home, on the job, and in school. Each type of writing is discussed and explained in a straightforward, helpful way; treating everyday tasks with as much respect as the more academic skills.

Beginning English Writing Skills is intended for high school, junior college, and adult education limited English proficient students. It is also for English as a foreign language students planning to live/work/function in an English-speaking environment, and for the many native speakers of English who need help mastering a variety of basic writing skills too often ignored in today's classrooms. The format of the book also makes *Beginning English Writing Skills* suitable for independent study, for students who want to improve their writing skills on their own without a formal language program.

For each type of writing, you will find:

1. a **Rationale** for doing this type of writing

2. a list of the **Materials Needed**

3. the **Skills Involved**

4. the **Important Vocabulary**

5. an **Example** of the kind of writing to be practiced

6. a step-by-step **Procedure** for doing the writing

7. a **Practice** activity—a real-life task involving the kind of writing that's been discussed.

In addition, most of the lessons include an evaluation process to measure the success of the written practice.

Beginning English Writing Skills is meant to be used as it best suits the user. Therefore, you can start at page one and follow through to the end; start in the middle and work backward and forward at will; or even start with the last chapter, if that's the one you need immediately. No matter where you begin, you will find that *Beginning English Writing Skills* is not only a guide but also an easy reference book, much the same as your dictionary is. You can turn to this book anytime for information about whatever type of writing you need to do. The book was written with your needs in mind. Enjoy.

Unit One

Notes and Messages

Leaving a Note

There are many times we want to leave a note for someone. For example, if you're leaving home when everyone else is sleeping and you won't be back at your usual time, you might want to leave a note so no one will worry about you. If you want to remind someone to do you a favor or to call you later, or to meet you at a certain time, you can leave that person a note.

Rationale

At times, it is more considerate to leave a note for someone than to disturb that person; for example, you could leave someone a note if you want that person to remember:

- you have an appointment together.

- that you won't be home for dinner.

- to pick up your clothes at the dry cleaners.

If you leave your message in writing, there's less chance the person will forget it—especially if he or she is half asleep or busy with something else and not listening carefully. Another good time to leave a note is when you have a message for someone who isn't at home or isn't available to talk to you. When you leave a note, you can be sure that you have let the person know your message.

Materials Needed

paper, pen or pencil

Skills Involved

organizing thoughts; giving specific information; using correct spelling, punctuation, capitalization, and abbreviations

Important Vocabulary

considerate thoughtful

disturb bother

do someone a favor help someone

note a short letter

organizing thoughts arranging information in a clear, logical order. A note that says *Meet me at 3 P.M. Pick up my clothes at the dry cleaners. I'll be in front of the post office* is not as clear as *Meet me at 3 P.M. in front of the post office. Please pick up my clothes at the dry cleaners first.*

pick up get

remind tell someone to remember

specific information facts and details; *at 3 P.M. in front of the post office* is specific information.

Examples

Mom,
I won't be home until 4:30. I'm going to the library after school with Kim.
Jean

Jean,
I'll be at the office until 5 P.M. The soup is on the stove. Please turn the burner on low at 4:30. See you later.
Mom

Bill,
Please pick me up in front of Brown's Dept. Store on Main St. at 4:45 P.M. I'll be waiting outside.

Tanya

Procedure ▼

1. Use a piece of paper that is large enough to be seen.

2. Organize your thoughts and then write down your message.

3. Be sure your handwriting—including your signature—is easy to read, especially if there are times, addresses, or directions involved.

4. Put your note where it will be seen by the person you want to read it. If the note is for a family member, you might want to tape it to the refrigerator or on the bathroom mirror or next to the telephone.

5. Read your note again. Be sure your message is clear.

Practice ▼

Now it's your turn.

Task: to leave a note for someone

Situation: You leave the house before your brother is awake. You want him to pick you up at your friend's house at 6 P.M. Think about what he needs to know, and write a note to leave for him. *Be sure to give him specific information.*

Did you remember to tell your brother:

- your friend's name?

- your friend's address and telephone number?

- directions to your friend's house?

If you forgot any of this information, you may still be waiting to be picked up!

Writing a Note

Most people don't realize how important notes are in their daily lives. Every day thousands of people write notes to thousands of others who read them, or try to. Sometimes note writers are in such a hurry that they forget to write so that others can understand their handwriting or their message. However, notes are just about the easiest thing to learn to write.

Rationale

Most of us write many, many notes in a lifetime. If you're in school now, for example, you might write a note to explain to your teacher why you didn't do a certain homework assignment (if you're too nervous to just speak to the teacher). You might want to be excused from school early one day, and if you're eighteen or older you can write your own note explaining why. Another type of note might even be a short letter of apology to someone you're too shy to face in person, such as a friend you've been rude to. If you have children, you may want to make an appointment to see your child's teacher, or you may need to write an "excuse" for your child's absence or a note requesting that your child be excused from some activity on a particular day.

Materials Needed

unlined stationery, envelope, pen

Skills Involved

organizing thoughts; giving specific information; using correct spelling, punctuation, capitalization, and abbreviations

Important Vocabulary

absence being away from someplace; for example, being away from school

apology saying you're sorry

closing a word or phrase used to end a letter. The closing is found just above the writer's signature and is always followed by a comma.

copy something that is exactly like something else; for example, if you want to have proof that you have written a certain note, you should make a copy of it to keep for yourself.

excuse reason given for something. For example, many schools want a written excuse when a student returns from an absence.

indented form a format for writing letters in which the first line of each paragraph is placed farther in from the margin than the salutation

margin the space that is left empty on the top, bottom, and sides of a page containing a note or other writing

modified block form a format for writing letters in which the margins are the same from the first line to the end. Nothing is indented. A blank space is left between paragraphs.

note a short letter

rude not polite

salutation the greeting in a letter, usually beginning with *Dear* followed by a person's name

Examples

a. Indented form

right margin

top margin

salutation

left margin

closing

bottom margin

> January 11, 19—
>
> Dear Mr. Garcia,
>
> Please excuse my daughter, Connie Ballou, at 1:45 P.M. today. We have an appointment with Dr. Anne Ache at 2 P.M. It was the only appointment we could get. Thank you.
>
> Sincerely,
> Mrs. Jane Ballou

b. Modified Block Form

right margin

top margin

salutation

left margin

closing

bottom margin

> March 15, 19—
>
> Dear Marco,
>
> I'm sorry I was so rude yesterday. I was nervous because of the big math test. When you asked to borrow my homework, I really got angry because I had worked so hard on it. Please call me later.
>
> Your friend,
> Ashok

Procedure ▼

1. Use a piece of unlined stationery. If your stationery is the fold-over kind, write on the inside.

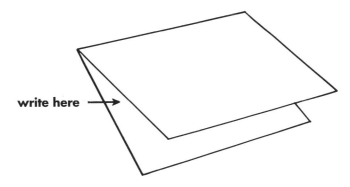

write here ⟶

2. Leave a margin on all four sides of the stationery.

3. Write the date in the upper right-hand corner.

June 9, 19—

4. Leave some space below the date. Then, starting at the left-hand margin, write *Dear* and the name of the person you're writing to. This is called the *salutation*. It is the greeting at the beginning of any note or letter. The first letter of the first word and the names of any people in the salutation should be capitalized. Put a comma after the salutation.

June 9, 19—

Dear Ms. Wang,

5. Below the salutation, begin your message. You can use modified block form or you can indent the first line.

> June 9, 19–
>
> Dear Ms. Wang,
> I'm sorry I didn't give you my homework today, but I was working on the floor and my dog came over and stepped on it and messed it all up. I didn't want to give you a dirty paper, but I promise I won't do my homework on the floor anymore.

6. Under the message, on the right, end your note with a word or phrase that shows respect and how you feel. *Sincerely* is a good word to use because it says that you really mean what you say. This word or phrase is called the *closing*. The first word of the closing should be capitalized. Put a comma after the closing.

7. Sign your name below the closing. When you write to a teacher, it's a good idea to use your complete name.

> Sincerely,
> Filomena Danang

The finished note should look something like this:

> June 9, 19–
>
> Dear Ms. Wang,
> I'm sorry I didn't give you my homework today, but I was working on the floor and my dog came over and stepped on it and messed it all up. I didn't want to give you a dirty paper, but I promise I won't do my homework on the floor anymore.
>
> Sincerely,
> Filomena Danang

8. Put the note in an envelope and write the person's name in the middle of the envelope.

> Ms. Wang

Practice ▼

Now it's your turn.

Task: to write a note to someone

Situation: You want to leave school early tomorrow because you have to go to the dentist. Write a note to the school principal, asking to be excused. Remember the form:

Remember to write carefully so the other person can read your handwriting easily. After you finish writing, read your note again to make sure you haven't made any mistakes.

3

Writing a Thank-You Note

We write thank-you notes for many reasons at different times in our lives. For example, you have just had a surprise birthday party. Guests brought gifts to your party, and out-of-town relatives sent gifts by mail. You thank people at the party, but you also want to write each one a note afterwards, naming the particular gift he or she gave you. Writing a thank-you note shows you appreciate the time, effort, and money spent by the person who brought or sent you a present. Of course, you could make phone calls or buy thank-you notes that say it already, but since someone thought enough of you to make or buy a gift, you'll want to show the same thoughtfulness.

You might write a thank-you note when someone has done something special for you. You want to show your appreciation, so you write a note thanking the person for being so kind.

Another occasion for writing thank-you notes might be when someone close to you has died. Friends visit you to help you in your time of sorrow. Later, you send notes thanking them for caring.

Rationale

Someone has taken the time, energy, and money to buy or make a gift for you or to show you in some nice way that you are special. To express your appreciation, you take the time and energy to thank the person with a short note, especially if:

- you received the person's gift by mail,

- you received many gifts at the same time and you want to let the giver know you are aware of and appreciate his or her particular gift, or

- the note is in response to a kindness or a special favor.

Materials Needed

unlined stationery, matching envelope, postage stamp, pen, dictionary to check spelling, correct name and complete address of the gift giver, information about the gift

Skills Involved

writing simple sentences; using correct punctuation, spelling, and capitalization; expressing thanks; showing gratitude by mentioning specific gift and something special about it

Important Vocabulary

closing a word or phrase used to end a letter. The closing is found just above the writer's signature and is always followed by a comma.

come in handy be useful

grateful thankful, appreciative

indented form a format for writing letters in which the first line of each paragraph is placed farther in from the margin than the salutation

margin the space that is left empty on the top, bottom, and sides of a page containing a note or other writing

matching envelope an envelope that is the right size and color for the stationery you are using

modified block form a format for writing letters in which the margins are the same from the first line to the end. Nothing is indented. A blank space is left between paragraphs.

note a short letter

return address the name and address of the person sending a note or letter

salutation the greeting in a letter, usually beginning with *Dear* followed by a person's name

Examples

a. Modified Block Form

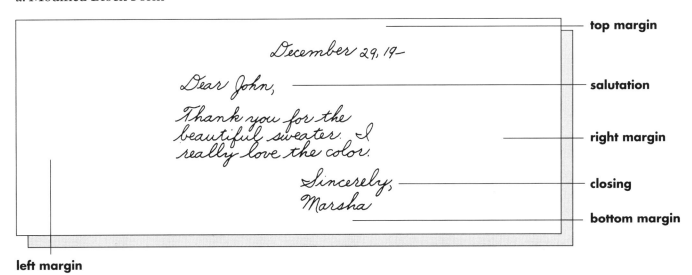

b. Indented Form

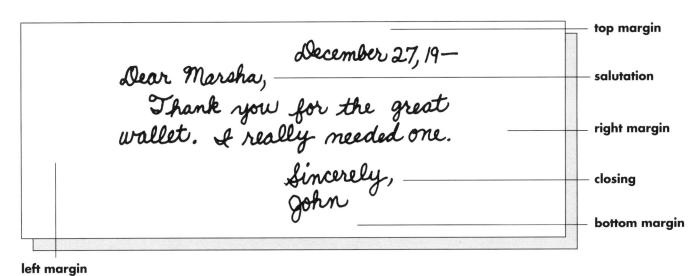

Procedure A: Writing the Letter ▼

1.   Use a piece of unlined stationery. If your stationery is the fold-over kind, write on the inside.

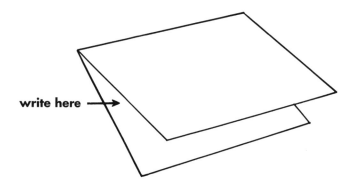

write here →

2.   Leave a margin on both sides of the stationery.

3.   Put the date in the upper right-hand corner.

June 11, 19–

4.   Leave some space below the date. Then, starting at the left-hand margin, write *Dear* and the name of the person you're writing to. This is called the *salutation*. It is the greeting at the beginning of any note or letter. The first letter of the first word and all names in the salutation should be capitalized. Put a comma after the salutation.

June 11, 19–

Dear Aunt Sally,

5. Below the salutation, begin your message. You can use block form or you can indent the first line. Thank the person by naming the gift and telling why it's useful or what you like about it. Look at these examples.

a.

> June 11, 19–
>
> Dear Aunt Sally,
> Thank you for the beautiful sweater. I love the color and I know it will keep me warm this winter.

b.

> Thank you for the book. I can't wait to read it.

c.

> Thank you for the check. I know it will come in handy.

6.   Under the message, on the right, end your note with a word or phrase that shows how you feel. *Sincerely* is a good word to use with friends or older people. You might want to say something stronger—for example, *With love* or *Fondly*—if you're writing to someone you're very close to. This word or phrase is called the *closing*. The first word of the closing should be capitalized. Put a comma after the closing.

7.   Sign your name below the closing. Since you're writing to a friend or a family member, your first name is all that's necessary.

This is what your letter might look like:

> *June 11, 19–*
>
> Dear Aunt Sally,
> Thank you for the beautiful sweater. I love the color. I know it will keep me warm this winter.
>
> Sincerely,
> Jim

Practice A ▼

Now it's your turn.

Task: to write a thank-you note

Situation: You have received a present from your cousin, who lives in another state. You want to let him know you received the gift and are very grateful. Remember the form:

```
                              _____

_____ ,

         _____

         _____

         _____

                    _____ ,

                    _____
```

Remember to write with a pen and to read your note after you finish writing it to make sure you haven't made mistakes.

Procedure B: Addressing the Envelope ▼

Now you must address the envelope. It is extremely important to use the correct name, address, and any special codes for the city, state, or country you're writing to.

1. Put your name and address in the upper left-hand corner of the envelope so that if the letter cannot be delivered for some reason, it will be returned to you. This is called the *return address*.

2. In the center of the envelope, write the name and address of the person you have written to. Put the name first, the number and street below that, and the city, state, and zip code on a third line. If there is an apartment number, it can go on the second line after the street name. If the letter is going to another country, be sure to put the name of the country on a fourth line.

3. Put a postage stamp in the upper right-hand corner. Be sure to use the right amount of postage, or the letter will not be delivered.

The finished envelope should look like this:

Jim Brown
425 E. Grant St. Apt. 11B
Lincoln, ND 74583

Ms. Sally Saucer
411 Ashburn Terrace
Denver, CO 54321

Practice B ▼

Now it's your turn.

Task: to address an envelope

Situation: You wrote a thank-you note to your cousin, who lives in another state, and now you need to address the envelope so you can mail it. Address the envelope.

Procedure C: Folding the Note ▼

1. If you have written your note on smaller stationery, use a matching envelope (one that is the appropriate size for the stationery). Smaller stationery is usually folded in half.

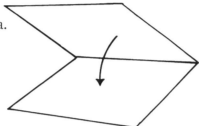

a.

2. If you are using typing paper ($8^1/2" \times 11"$), fold your paper in thirds. Start by folding the bottom edge up above the middle b. Then fold the top down over the middle fold c. Use a "business size" envelope.

b.

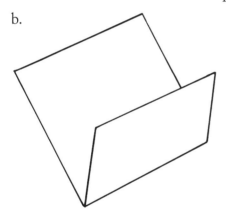

c.

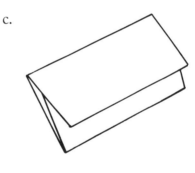

Practice C ▼

Now it's your turn.

Task: to fold your note properly

Situation: You have proofread your note, checking the spelling, punctuation, names, and addresses. Your envelope is addressed. Fold your letter and put it in the envelope.

Taking a Message

The telephone rings. You are the only one there to answer it. The call is for someone else. You say you'll "take a message."

Rationale

If someone calls for you when you aren't home or at work and another person answers the phone, you'd probably like to know who called you, when, and why. The person for whom you're taking a message would like to know the same things.

Materials Needed

paper, pen or pencil

Skills Involved

listening comprehension; asking the right questions; taking notes; knowing how to use abbreviations

Important Vocabulary

abbreviation a shortened form of a word; for example, *Mr.* for *Mister*, *appt.* for *appointment*

can (may) *Can* really means "Am I able to?" *May* really means "Do I have your permission to?" However, *can* is acceptable in informal or colloquial speech when asking permission, as in "Can I take a message?"

hold on wait a minute; don't hang up the phone. This expression is often used when you want the person to wait while you get paper and pencil to take a message.

legible clear and easy to read

take a message write down what someone is telling you, usually to give it to someone else

text written words

Example

Look at this conversation and pretend it is taking place over the telephone.

YOU:	Hello.
LARRY HARP:	Hello. May I speak to Mr. Ross, please?
YOU:	I'm sorry. He's not here right now. Can (May) I take a message? (or, Would you like to leave a message?)
LARRY HARP:	Yes. This is Larry Harp. I had an appointment with Mr. Ross for tomorrow morning at 9 A.M. I want to change the appointment. Please have him call me.
YOU:	Would you spell your last name for me, please?
LARRY HARP:	Harp. H-A-R-P as in Peter.
YOU:	What's your phone number, Mr. Harp?
LARRY HARP:	555-0632.
YOU:	555-0632? Let me be sure I have the correct information. You want to change your appointment for tomorrow morning and you want Mr. Ross to call you.
LARRY HARP:	Right.
YOU:	Okay, I'll give him the message.
LARRY HARP:	Thank you. Good-bye.
YOU:	Bye.

What notes would you write down during the conversation? Look at this example:

> *Mr. Ross- Mr. Harp- 3:25 P.M.*
> *wants change appt. for tom.*
> *morn. Call 555-0632.*

Rewrite the message so Mr. Ross will understand it if you're not there to explain it:

> *Mr. Ross,*
> *Mr. Harp called at*
> *3:25 P.M. Wants to change*
> *appt. for tomorrow A.M.*
> *Call him at 555-0632.*
> *Bill Williams*

If Mr. Ross is your father, change the salutation to *Dear Dad*, and sign your first name only.

Procedure ▼

1. It's important to have paper and a pen or pencil near the phone for taking messages. If you don't have any, ask the person who has called to please "hold on" while you get what you need. Don't trust your memory alone. You might forget an important part of the message, like the phone number, or you might not get to see the person to deliver the message. Here are some polite expressions you can use on the phone.

   - She's not here right now. Please hold on while I get a pen.
   - Would you like to leave a message?
   - Just one moment. I'll get a piece of paper... Now, what is your message, please?

2. As you listen and take notes, use abbreviations that will be easy for you to remember when it's time to write the message out. Some easy ones include the following:

    A.M. morning
    aft. afternoon
    appt. appointment
    Ave. Avenue
    Dr. Doctor
    eve. evening
    Mr. Mr.
    Ms. Miss/Mrs.
    P.M. afternoon or evening (used with a number)
    St. Street
    w/ with
    # number
    & and

    It helps to be familiar with common abbreviations of cities, states, and countries if you have to take messages at work. Abbreviations for the days and months are also useful to know.

3. As you listen to the caller and take notes, write only the necessary words. You can always write the message over again once you have the important facts. (See the notes about the example conversation on page 24.)

4. Don't be afraid to ask the caller to repeat information, including how to spell his or her name. If you hear letters you're not sure of, use a familiar word to identify each letter, "Is that *F* as in *Frank*?"

5. Repeat the message to the caller to be sure you've got the correct information.

6. Write out the message and read it over before you leave it. Is it clear? Is it legible? Will the receiver understand it even if you're not there to explain it? Messages do not have to be written in complete sentences. You can use abbreviations as long as you make the message clear.

7. Be sure to sign the message and tell what time you answered the phone.

8. Leave the message in a place where you're sure it will be seen by the appropriate person.

Practice ▼

Now it's your turn.

Task: to take a telephone message for someone else

Situation: You are working in a store. The owner has gone out, asking you to take any messages. The telephone rings. Your teacher will play the conversation for you. Listen to it* and take notes. What message would you leave for Mr. Patel?

Take notes here as you listen to the caller:

Write your message here:

*Your teacher will read or play the conversation for you. However, the text of the conversation is printed on page 28. If you are studying independently, try to find someone to read it to you so you can practice taking notes in a listening situation. If there is no one to read the conversation to you, look at the text and take notes from it, remembering that this is not quite the same as hearing the words.

Did your message look something like this?

> Mr. Patel,
>
> Mrs. Sung from Apt. 14L next door called at 2 P.M. You sent her the wrong order. She wants 3 cans of cola and 2 gallons of milk. She rec'd 2 cans of cola + 3 gallons of milk. I told her you'd call her at 555-8797 as soon as you came back.
>
> Naresh

Note that *and* (&) and *received* (rec'd) can be abbreviated. Your message could be even shorter:

> Mr. Patel,
>
> Mrs. Sung, Apt. 14L next door, wants 3 cans cola, 2 gallons milk. You sent the opposite. Told her you'd call (555-8797) when you came back.
>
> Naresh
> 2 P.M. Tues.

What's important is to include the name, address, and phone number of the caller, the time of the call, and the message.

Transcript of a telephone call for use in Practice, page 26.

YOU:	Hello.
CALLER:	This is Mrs. Sung. Let me speak to Mr. Patel, please.
YOU:	I'm sorry. Mr. Patel isn't here right now. Can I take a message?
CALLER:	Yes. I ordered three cans of cola and two gallons of milk. He sent me two cans of cola and three gallons of milk. I want him to send me the correct order. I can't come to the store because my baby is sick.
YOU:	Hold on a minute, please. How do you spell your name?
CALLER:	S-U-N-G.
YOU:	Is that *F* as in *Frank?*
CALLER:	No, *S* as in *soda.* S-U-N as in Nancy-G.
YOU:	Okay, Mrs. Sung. Now, what is the correct order?
CALLER:	Three cans of cola and two gallons of milk. He sent me . . .
YOU:	Okay, Mrs. Sung. I'll give Mr. Patel the message. I'm sure he'll correct the mistake. Where do you live?
CALLER:	I live right next door in apartment 14L.
YOU:	Can I have your telephone number, please?
CALLER:	555-8797.
YOU:	555-8797. Mr. Patel will take care of it as soon as he comes back.
CALLER:	Thank you. I hope he gets back soon.
YOU:	Good-bye, Mrs. Sung.

Unit Two

Forms and Identification

Applying for a Social Security Card

A Social Security card is probably one of the most important means of identification you can have in the United States. Others may have the same name as you, the same birthday, the same address, but no one can have the same Social Security number. You need a Social Security card to work legally in the United States. You can apply for a Social Security number if you are in this country legally, even if you are not eligible to work. In the United States, parents are encouraged to get Social Security cards for their children as soon as they are born. Applications are available at Social Security agencies in cities throughout the United States.

Rationale

If you are planning to live in the United States, you will need a Social Security card as a means of identification to work legally. People who work here must pay taxes and have a certain amount of money taken out of their paycheck for Social Security. This money is held by the United States government. When people reach a certain age, they can start collecting Social Security from the government—a certain amount of money each month for the rest of their lives, based on the amount they have paid in over the years.

Materials Needed

typewriter or pen, information from birth certificate or passport and from Form I-151 or I-551 or Form I-94. When applying for your actual Social Security card, remember that only an original birth certificate or passport and documents given to you by the INS (Immigration and

Naturalization Services) are acceptable. No photocopies of any documents are accepted. Examples of INS documents are your Alien Registration Receipt Card (Form I-151 or I-551) or Form I-94. You must bring these papers to your local Social Security office and apply in person.

Skills Involved

reading; following directions; accuracy

Important Vocabulary

abbreviate to make shorter; to abbreviate *street*, we write *St.*

adoptive parent not a birth parent; someone who becomes a parent by law

authorized given permission for. When you get a Social Security card, it is a way of saying you are given permission by the government to work in the United States.

deliberately on purpose. If you do something deliberately, you know what you are doing. It is not an accident.

documents official papers such as a passport, a birth certificate, a marriage license

false not true. If you were born in Poland and you say you were born in France, you are giving false information.

furnishing giving, as in furnishing (giving) your correct address

legal guardian the person the law has said is in charge of you until you reach a certain age

mailing address the address where you want to receive your mail. It can be your home, a post office box, or a place where you are living temporarily (for a while).

middle name the name between your first and last names. Not everyone has a middle name.

original the first. Your original birth certificate is the first one that was issued to you. Everything else may be copies.

photocopies copies of the original

PO box Some people receive their mail in a special box at the Post Office (PO)

previously before; you may live in the United States now, but where did you live previously?

race/ethnic description a division of people for purposes of discussion or identification based on certain physical characteristics, national origins with similar cultures. *Caucasian* and *Asian* are often used as examples of race, *Hispanic* and *Native American* as examples of ethnic origins.

restricted limited. If work is restricted, it means there are limits to how many hours a person can work, or how much money the person can earn, or at what age the person can work, etc.

rural route no. People who live in very rural areas where there aren't too many people, and houses are miles apart, often have a rural route number where their mail is delivered. There may be several mailboxes on a rural route and people have to drive to them to get their mail.

sex gender; male (man or boy) or female, (woman or girl)

signature the way you sign your name, not print it. Everyone's signature is different.

Social Security money for retirement. In the United States, working people pay money into a national Social Security system so that they will receive money when they reach a certain age and no longer wish to/are able to work. If a working person dies before that time, the Social Security benefits go to the immediate family.

voluntary by choice. When you provide voluntary information, you do it because you want to, not because you have to.

Example

SOCIAL SECURITY ADMINISTRATION
Application for a Social Security Card

Form Approved
OMB No. 0960-0066

INSTRUCTIONS
- Please read "How To Complete This Form" on page 2.
- Print or type using black or blue ink. DO NOT USE PENCIL.
- After you complete this form, take or mail it along with the required documents to your nearest Social Security office.
- If you are completing this form for someone else, answer the questions as they apply to that person. Then, sign your name in question 16.

1 NAME To Be Shown On Card

FIRST *TORY*   FULL MIDDLE NAME *CHELSEA*   LAST *SHELDON*

FULL NAME AT BIRTH IF OTHER THAN ABOVE

FIRST *TORY*   FULL MIDDLE NAME   LAST *SHELDON de VEGA*

OTHER NAMES USED

2 MAILING ADDRESS Do Not Abbreviate

1334 D SPERBER ROAD
STREET ADDRESS, APT. NO., PO BOX, RURAL ROUTE NO.

CITY *LAKE WORTH*   STATE *FLORIDA*   ZIP CODE *33333*

3 CITIZENSHIP (Check One)
- [ ] U.S. Citizen
- [ ] Legal Alien Allowed To Work
- [ ] Legal Alien Not Allowed To Work
- [X] Foreign Student Allowed Restricted Employment
- [ ] Conditionally Legalized Alien Allowed To Work
- [ ] Other (See Instructions On Page 2)

4 SEX
- [ ] Male
- [X] Female

5 RACE/ETHNIC DESCRIPTION (Check One Only—Voluntary)
- [ ] Asian, Asian-American Or Pacific Islander
- [ ] Hispanic
- [ ] Black (Not Hispanic)
- [ ] North American Indian Or Alaskan Native
- [X] White (Not Hispanic)

6 DATE OF BIRTH *12 12 1980* MONTH DAY YEAR

7 PLACE OF BIRTH (Do Not Abbreviate) CITY *San Jose* STATE OR FOREIGN COUNTRY *Costa Rica*

Office Use Only FCI

8 MOTHER'S MAIDEN NAME FIRST *RUTH* FULL MIDDLE NAME *JEAN* LAST NAME AT HER BIRTH *VEGA*

9 FATHER'S NAME FIRST *RICARDO* FULL MIDDLE NAME LAST *SHELDON*

10 Has the person in item 1 ever received a Social Security number before?
- [ ] Yes (If "yes", answer questions 11-13.)
- [X] No (If "no", go on to question 14.)
- [ ] Don't Know (If "don't know", go on to question 14.)

11 Enter the Social Security number previously assigned to the person listed in item 1.

☐☐☐–☐☐–☐☐☐☐

12 Enter the name shown on the most recent Social Security card issued for the person listed in item 1.

FIRST   MIDDLE   LAST

13 Enter any different date of birth if used on an earlier application for a card. MONTH DAY YEAR

14 TODAY'S DATE *10 9 9* MONTH DAY YEAR

15 DAYTIME PHONE NUMBER AREA CODE *(561) 654 3210*

DELIBERATELY FURNISHING (OR CAUSING TO BE FURNISHED) FALSE INFORMATION ON THIS APPLICATION IS A CRIME PUNISHABLE BY FINE OR IMPRISONMENT, OR BOTH.

16 YOUR SIGNATURE
Tony Sheldon

17 YOUR RELATIONSHIP TO THE PERSON IN ITEM 1 IS:
- [X] Self
- [ ] Natural Or Adoptive Parent
- [ ] Legal Guardian
- [ ] Other (Specify)

DO NOT WRITE BELOW THIS LINE (FOR SSA USE ONLY)				
NPN	DOC	NTI	CAN	ITV
PBC	EVI	EVA	EVC	PRA	NWR	DNR	UNIT
EVIDENCE SUBMITTED				SIGNATURE AND TITLE OF EMPLOYEE(S) REVIEWING EVIDENCE AND/OR CONDUCTING INTERVIEW

DATE

DCL   DATE

Procedure ▼

1. Read everything carefully before writing anything. Ask questions if you are not sure of something.

2. Be sure you have all the necessary information and that it matches (is the same as) the information on your birth certificate and other documents (legal papers.)

3. Where it says NAME TO BE SHOWN ON CARD, be sure to print your name exactly as you want it to appear on your Social Security card.

    If the name on your birth certificate is different from the name you use now, write the name from your birth certificate where it says FULL NAME AT BIRTH IF OTHER THAN ABOVE.

    If your name is not different, draw a line across to show you have answered.

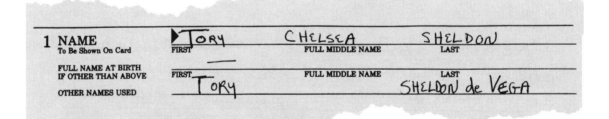

4. Where it says MAILING ADDRESS, be sure to print the address of the place where you want to receive your mail, whether it's at your home, a post office box number, or elsewhere. Be sure to include the correct zip code. If you live in an apartment building, it is very important to include the exact apartment number. Follow directions; do not abbreviate.

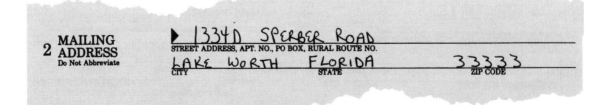

5. Put an X in the correct box for CITIZENSHIP. Be sure to answer honestly. Ask questions if you are not sure which box to check. Notice that on Tory's application, she has checked "Foreign Student Allowed Restricted Employment." This means Tory is a student in the United States and can only apply for certain types of jobs for a certain number of hours per week or for a certain length of time while she is in this country as a student. If you are a legal alien not allowed to work for any reason (your age, for example), remember to fill out a new application when your status changes (when you are able to work). If you don't, when you begin work and it is reported to the INS, you could have a problem.

6. You do not have to enter your RACE/ETHNIC DESCRIPTION. If you volunteer to answer, read each category before checking the one that best identifies you.

7. When filling in DATE OF BIRTH, write the number of the month, then the day, then the year. When filling in PLACE OF BIRTH, do not abbreviate the city, state, or country where you were born.

8. In the United States, it is not unusual for a woman to stop using her maiden name (the last name she has had since birth) when she gets married. Many women take the last name of their husband when they get married. Their maiden name becomes another form of identification, so it is important to write your mother's maiden name where it says LAST NAME AT HER BIRTH.

9. Be sure to write your father's full name, even if he is deceased (dead) or does not live with you.

10. If you have never applied for a Social Security card before, put an X in question 10 and do not answer numbers 11, 12, and 13.

11. Where it says TODAY'S DATE, notice again you must write the month, then the day and year. Your DAYTIME PHONE NUMBER is very important. Be sure to include the area code.

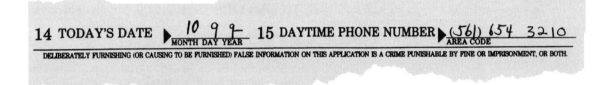

12. Write your signature exactly as you sign it. Do not print or type your signature.

13. If you are filling out this application for yourself, put an X in the box that says SELF. If you are filling out the application for someone else, be sure to read the directions for necessary documents, etc.

14. Read the entire application again.

    • Did you answer all the questions or draw a line to show you have read them?

    • Does the information you've given match the information on the documents you will have to show to get your Social Security card?

    • Is the information legible (easy to read)?

    • Did you sign and date the application?

Congratulations. You are ready to apply for your Social Security card.

Practice ▼

Now it's your turn.

Task: to fill out an application for a Social Security card

Situation: You plan to stay in the United States, to make it your legal residence, and to get a job as soon as possible. You need to have a Social Security card to work legally.

SOCIAL SECURITY ADMINISTRATION
Application for a Social Security Card

Form Approved
OMB No. 0960-0066

INSTRUCTIONS
- Please read "How To Complete This Form" on page 2.
- Print or type using black or blue ink. DO NOT USE PENCIL.
- After you complete this form, take or mail it along with the required documents to your nearest Social Security office.
- If you are completing this form for someone else, answer the questions as they apply to that person. Then, sign your name in question 16.

1 NAME To Be Shown On Card — FIRST / FULL MIDDLE NAME / LAST

FULL NAME AT BIRTH IF OTHER THAN ABOVE — FIRST / FULL MIDDLE NAME / LAST

OTHER NAMES USED

2 MAILING ADDRESS Do Not Abbreviate — STREET ADDRESS, APT. NO., PO BOX, RURAL ROUTE NO.

CITY / STATE / ZIP CODE

3 CITIZENSHIP (Check One) — ☐ U.S. Citizen ☐ Legal Alien Allowed To Work ☐ Legal Alien Not Allowed To Work ☐ Foreign Student Allowed Restricted Employment ☐ Conditionally Legalized Alien Allowed To Work ☐ Other (See Instructions On Page 2)

4 SEX — ☐ Male ☐ Female

5 RACE/ETHNIC DESCRIPTION (Check One Only—Voluntary) — ☐ Asian, Asian-American Or Pacific Islander ☐ Hispanic ☐ Black (Not Hispanic) ☐ North American Indian Or Alaskan Native ☐ White (Not Hispanic)

6 DATE OF BIRTH — MONTH DAY YEAR

7 PLACE OF BIRTH (Do Not Abbreviate) — CITY / STATE OR FOREIGN COUNTRY / FCI — Office Use Only

8 MOTHER'S MAIDEN NAME — FIRST / FULL MIDDLE NAME / LAST NAME AT HER BIRTH

9 FATHER'S NAME — FIRST / FULL MIDDLE NAME / LAST

10 Has the person in item 1 ever received a Social Security number before?
☐ Yes (If "yes", answer questions 11-13.) ☐ No (If "no", go on to question 14.) ☐ Don't Know (If "don't know", go on to question 14.)

11 Enter the Social Security number previously assigned to the person listed in item 1.
☐☐☐ – ☐☐ – ☐☐☐☐

12 Enter the name shown on the most recent Social Security card issued for the person listed in item 1.
FIRST / MIDDLE / LAST

13 Enter any different date of birth if used on an earlier application for a card. MONTH DAY YEAR

14 TODAY'S DATE ▶ MONTH DAY YEAR   **15 DAYTIME PHONE NUMBER** ▶ AREA CODE

DELIBERATELY FURNISHING (OR CAUSING TO BE FURNISHED) FALSE INFORMATION ON THIS APPLICATION IS A CRIME PUNISHABLE BY FINE OR IMPRISONMENT, OR BOTH.

16 YOUR SIGNATURE ▶

17 YOUR RELATIONSHIP TO THE PERSON IN ITEM 1 IS:
☐ Self ☐ Natural Or Adoptive Parent ☐ Legal Guardian ☐ Other (Specify)

DO NOT WRITE BELOW THIS LINE (FOR SSA USE ONLY)

NPN		DOC	NTI	CAN		ITV
PBC	EVI	EVA	EVC	PRA	NWR	DNR	UNIT

EVIDENCE SUBMITTED

SIGNATURE AND TITLE OF EMPLOYEE(S) REVIEWING EVIDENCE AND/OR CONDUCTING INTERVIEW

DATE

DCL   DATE

Form SS-5 (9/89)   3

When you finish filling out your application, go back to item 14 under Procedure. Did you complete everything? Keep this application to help you when you go to the Social Security office nearest you to apply for your card. Remember to bring all the necessary documents with you. Good luck.

Filling Out a Form W-4

You have a Social Security card. Now you will need to find a job, or maybe you already have one. Either way, you must be ready to fill out Form W-4, the "Employee's Withholding Allowance Certificate." It's the piece of paper that goes to the federal government, telling them how many dependents you claim and a lot of other personal information that has to do with paying income tax. There's a lot of printed material on Form W-4, but if you read it carefully and follow the directions, you should have no problem. You should read every word carefully, for your own protection, because there is a lot to know. For example, the more dependents you have, the less taxes are taken out of each paycheck. If you claim fewer dependents than you have, you may get a tax refund at the end of the tax year. If you claim too many dependents, you may have to pay a penalty at the end of the tax year for not paying enough taxes.

Rationale

If you are employed legally in this country, you must fill out a Form W-4. This form will establish how much money is withheld from your paycheck for taxes and is used when completing your tax form (Form 1040) by April 15th of each year.

Materials Needed

dark pen, typewriter (optional), Form W-4, necessary information to complete W-4, including your Social Security number.

Skills Involved

comprehension; collecting necessary information

Important Vocabulary

certificate a piece of paper containing specific information on a subject

certify say that something is true (see **claim**)

claim declare to be true (see **certify**)

dependents people you take care of financially

deducted taken away from a total expense

deductions amounts allowed to be subtracted from income

employed working

employee worker

employer the person the employee works for. The employer pays the employee.

entitled to have the right to something

establish make official

exempt free from something (a rule, a duty, or a payment)

expenses living costs that can be deducted from income

income tax tax paid on money earned, after deductions have been taken

IRS Internal Revenue Service; government organization that collects federal taxes, makes refunds, etc.

legally according to the law

penalty a sum of money that must be paid if you didn't pay the right amount of tax owed

perjury deliberately giving false information on your tax return

refund money that's returned

single not married

spouse husband or wife, person you are married to

tax return the paper filed by April 15th of every year showing income, expenses, etc.

withholding allowance the number of dependents used to determine the amount of money taken out of each paycheck for tax purposes

Example

FORM W-4 _____
Personal Allowances Worksheet
A. Enter "1" for **yourself** if no one else can claim you as a dependent A---1----
        (You are single and have only one job; or   )
B. Enter "1" if   (You are married, have only one job, and your spouse) B---1----
       (does not work; or   )
       (Your wages from a second job or your spouse's wages)
       ((or the total of both) are $1,000.00 or less.   )
C. Enter "1" for your **spouse**. But, you may choose to enter -0- if you are
    married and have either a working spouse or more than one job (this may
    help you avoid having too little tax withheld)... C----0-----
D. Enter number of **dependents** (other than your spouse or yourself) you will
    claim on your tax return...D---0------
E. Enter "1" if you will file as **head of household** on your tax return.............E---0------
       (see conditions umder Head of Household above)
F. Enter "1" if you have at least $1500.00 of **child** or **dependent care**
    expenses for which you plan to claim a credit.................................F----0-----
G. Add lines A through F and enter total here. Note: This amount may be G----2-----
    different from the number of exemptions you claim on your return
Enter the number from line G on line 5 of Form W-4 below.

---------Cut here and give the certificate to your employer. Keep the top portion for your records.----------
Form W-4   **Employee's Withholding Allowance Certificate** | **199-**
MARNIE   *P.*   *SEIDMAN*   *153-15-1531* |
1 Type or print your first name and middle initial   Last name   2 Your social security number

16 MAIN STREET
Home address (number and street or rural route)   3 ☒single ☐ married ☐married but withhold at
                                       higher Single rate
                           Note: if married, but legally separated or spouse is a
                           nonresident alien, check the Single box
AUSTIN, TX 78372
City or town, state and ZIP code   4 If your last name differs from that on your social
                                 security card, check here and call 1 800-772-1213
                                 for a new card.. ☐
5 Total number of allowances you are claiming (from line G above) .... |5| 2
6 Additional amount, if any, you want withheld from each paycheck .... |6| $0.00
7 I claim exemption from withholding for 199-, and I certify that I meet
    BOTH of the following conditions for exemption:
        Last year I had a right to a refund of ALL Federal Income tax withheld because I
        had NO tax liability; AND
        This year I expect a refund of ALL Federal Income tax withheld because I expect
        to have NO tax liability.
    If you meet both conditions, enter EXEMPT here................................... |7|

Under penalty of perjury, I certify that I am entitled to the number of withholding allowances claimed on
this certificate or entitled to claim exempt status.

Employee's signature   *Marnie Seidman*   Date _____

8 Employer's name and address (Employer: Complete 8 and 10 only if sending to IRS)	9 Office code	10 Employer identification number

Procedure ▼

If possible, read and discuss the Form W-4 with someone who is familiar with it. Make a list of questions for items you don't understand.

Fill out the form in pencil first so you can erase any mistakes. Follow the directions step by step:

A.   If you earn a salary and no one else claims you as a deduction, write 1 on line A. Remember to refer back to the example for help.

B.   1.   Are you single (not married)? Write 1 on line B.

2.   If you are married, have only one job, and your spouse (husband or wife) doesn't work, you can also write 1 on line B.

3.   If your wages (money earned) from a second job or your spouse's wages (or the total of both) are $1,000 or less, you can also write 1 on line B.

C.   Enter 1 for your spouse on line C. If you are married and your spouse is working or you have more than one job, you may want to enter "0" so you don't have too little tax withheld. Otherwise, when you file your income tax, you will have to pay any money the government says you owe because of this other income.

D.   On line D, write the number of dependents (other than your spouse or yourself) you want to claim on your tax return. This would include minor children living at home, or parents who live with you and whom you support, for example.

E.   Enter 1 on Line E if you are the head of your household (unmarried and paying more than 50% of the costs of keeping up a home for yourself and your dependents or other qualifying individuals). You may want to ask someone who works with taxes about this.

F.   If you have child or dependent care expenses of at least $1,500 a year and plan to claim a credit for this expense, write 1 on line F.

G.   Add lines A through F and enter the total on line G.

Stop here and enter the number from line G on line 5 of Form W-4 below. See the example. This top part of the form, Personal Allowances Worksheet, is for you to keep. Put it in a safe place so you can use it when you are making out your income tax returns.

When your employer gives you the Employee's Withholding Allowance Certificate, Form W-4, it will take you very little time to fill it in:

1. Follow the directions and write your first name, middle initial if you have a middle name, and last name. On the line below, write your address, putting the number and then the street or rural route number, if that is part of your address. On the line below that write the city or town, state, and ZIP code. See the Example on page 42.

2. Where it says 2, write your Social Security number exactly as it appears on your card.

3. Put a check in the appropriate box telling whether you are single, married, or married but want tax withheld at the single rate so you will get more money back at the end of the tax year. Notice the small print that says if you are married but legally separated, or your spouse is a nonresident alien (not living in the United States), you should check the Single box.

4. If your last name is different from the name on your Social Security card, check the box in number 4 and call the number listed for a new card.

5. This should be the same number you have written on line G of your Personal Allowances Worksheet.

6. If you want more money withheld from your paycheck, write the amount in number 6, next to the $.

7. If you are just starting to work in the United States, you probably won't write anything on line 7. If you had no federal income tax withheld last year and you expect to have no tax liability (owe any taxes) this year, then you can claim exemption. You must meet both conditions. Obviously, if you didn't work or pay taxes in the United States last year, you don't meet the first requirement. Remember that you must answer honestly or you can be punished for lying (committing perjury).

8. Sign your name as it will appear on your paycheck and tax statements (it should be the same as your name on your Social Security card) and write the date.

9. Your employer will fill out the bottom line of Form W-4.

10. Remember to use the example whenever you want to be sure you are following directions. But remember, too, to put in the numbers that are correct for you. Don't copy the numbers in the example. They are for Marnie Seidman.

Practice ▼

Now it's your turn.

Task: to fill out a Form W-4

Situation: You have just gotten a job. Good luck! Your new employer has just given you a Form W-4 to fill out so you can begin work. You know what to do!

Personal Allowances Worksheet

A Enter "1" for **yourself** if no one else can claim you as a dependent . . . . **A** ____

B Enter "1" if:
- You are single and have only one job; or
- You are married, have only one job, and your spouse does not work; or
- Your wages from a second job or your spouse's wages (or the total of both) are $1,000 or less.   . . **B** ____

C Enter "1" for your **spouse**. But, you may choose to enter -0- if you are married and have either a working spouse or more than one job. (This may help you avoid having too little tax withheld.). . . . . **C** ____

D Enter number of **dependents** (other than your spouse or yourself) you will claim on your tax return . . . **D** ____

E Enter "1" if you will file as **head of household** on your tax return (see conditions under **Head of household** above) . **E** ____

F Enter "1" if you have at least $1,500 of **child or dependent care expenses** for which you plan to claim a credit . . **F** ____

G **New—Child Tax Credit:** • If your total income will be between $16,500 and $47,000 ($21,000 and $60,000 if married), enter "1" for each eligible child. • If your total income will be between $47,000 and $80,000 ($60,000 and $115,000 if married), enter "1" if you have two or three eligible children, or enter "2" if you have four or more . . . . **G** ____

H Add lines A through G and enter total here. **Note:** This amount may be different from the number of exemptions you claim on your return. ► **H** ____

For accuracy, complete all worksheets that apply.	• If you plan to **itemize or claim adjustments to income** and want to reduce your withholding, see the Deductions and Adjustments Worksheet on page 2.
	• If you are **single**, have **more than one job**, and your combined earnings from all jobs exceed $32,000 OR if you are **married** and have a **working spouse or more than one job**, and the combined earnings from all jobs exceed $55,000, see the Two-Earner/Two-Job Worksheet on page 2 to avoid having too little tax withheld.
	• If **neither** of the above situations applies, **stop here** and enter the number from line H on line 5 of Form W-4 below.

- **Cut here and give the certificate to your employer. Keep the top part for your records.** - - - - - - - - - - - - - - - - - - -

Form **W-4** Department of the Treasury Internal Revenue Service	**Employee's Withholding Allowance Certificate** ► **For Privacy Act and Paperwork Reduction Act Notice, see page 2.**	OMB No. 1545-0010 **1998**

1 Type or print your first name and middle initial	Last name	**2** Your social security number

Home address (number and street or rural route)	**3** ☐ Single ☐ Married ☐ Married, but withhold at higher Single rate. **Note:** *If married, but legally separated, or spouse is a nonresident alien, check the Single box.*
City or town, state, and ZIP code	**4** If your last name differs from that on your social security card, check here and call 1-800-772-1213 for a new card . . . . . . ► ☐

5 Total number of allowances you are claiming (from line H above or from the worksheets on page 2 if they apply) . | **5** |

6 Additional amount, if any, you want withheld from each paycheck . . . . | **6** $

7 I claim exemption from withholding for 1998, and I certify that I meet **BOTH** of the following conditions for exemption:
- Last year I had a right to a refund of **ALL** Federal income tax withheld because I had **NO** tax liability **AND**
- This year I expect a refund of **ALL** Federal income tax withheld because I expect to have **NO** tax liability.

If you meet both conditions, enter "EXEMPT" here . . . . ► | **7** |

Under penalties of perjury, I certify that I am entitled to the number of withholding allowances claimed on this certificate or entitled to claim exempt status.

Employee's signature ► | **Date ►** _____ , 19___

8 Employer's name and address (Employer: Complete 8 and 10 only if sending to the IRS)	**9** Office code (optional)	**10** Employer identification number

Cat. No. 10220Q

Applying for a Driver's License

Almost everyone wants to drive a car today. As soon as they're of age, young people apply for their learner's permit. Many high schools have driver education programs so students can become responsible drivers and can be ready to pass their driver's test as soon as they reach legal age. (Legal age for getting a driver's license varies in the 50 states.) Because laws are different in each state, it is important to understand the rules in your state, especially if you are applying for your first driver's license. If you have a driver's license from another state or another country, you must check with your local Department of Motor Vehicles to see what procedure to follow.

Rationale

You must have a driver's license to drive legally in this country. Every state has a Department of Motor Vehicles where you can get an application. Once you have passed the road test, an eye test, and any written test given in your state, you can apply for a driver's license that is valid all over the United States and in many other countries you may visit. If you move to another state, you must get a new driver's license there within a certain period of time. You must surrender (give back) the license from the state you no longer live in.

Materials Needed

pen, identification showing name, legal address, age; marriage certificate or other document showing why your surname (last name) is different from that on the birth certificate; proof that you have passed road test, eye test, written test; eyeglasses, if needed for driving; form of payment for license

Skills Involved

reading; following directions; driving skill; understanding rules of the road; good vision (with or without eyeglasses)

Important Vocabulary

certify declare that something is true

convulsive disorder epilepsy or any other disorder that would cause violent shaking or fainting and make it difficult or unsafe to drive

county a geographic area in a state for governing purposes, usually a group of neighboring cities and towns

duplicate an exact copy, the same thing

eye test a test that is given to be sure you can see well enough to drive. If you wear eyeglasses, be sure to have them with you.

height (feet, inches) how tall you are in feet (ft) and inches (in)

initial first. Your initial driver's license is your first one. Your initials are the first letters of your first, middle, and last names.

mailing address the place where you receive your mail. It could be at home or at a post office box number, for example.

marriage certificate document showing your maiden name (last name before marriage), date and place of marriage. Necessary only if there has been a change in your surname (last name.) Usually necessary only for women, who often change their last name to that of their husband.

permit government permission. If you are getting your very first driver's license, you must first have a learner's permit, which gives you permission to practice driving with a licensed driver in the front seat next to you. You obtain the permit at the Department of Motor Vehicles the same way you apply for your license. The age for permits can be different from state to state.

privilege a special right or advantage. If you are found guilty of breaking the law while driving, your driving privileges can be suspended (taken away).

renewal make new again. A driver's license is good for a certain period of time. If you already have a driver's license, you can apply for a renewal when that time ends.

road test a test showing that you know how to drive and that you understand the rules of the road. You will usually get a date and time to take your test with a licensed member of the Department of Motor Vehicles, who will mark you on your ability to drive safely and to obey the law. You must pass this test in order to get a driver's license.

rural route people who live on farms or in less populated areas often have a mailbox not too close to their home. *Rural* means small village or countryside.

sex gender; male (boys, men) or female (girls, women)

Social Security number an important form of identification. You cannot legally work in this country without a Social Security number, and it is used by motor vehicle agencies and others to be sure there are no mistakes made because more than one person might have the same name, same address, or same birthdate. No two people have the same Social Security number.

suspended taken away for a period of time. If your driver's license is suspended, it means you cannot drive legally until it is given back to you. If a license is suspended, there is a record of it that any police officer can see if you are stopped for a violation (doing something wrong while driving) and have to show your driver's license.

valid legal; approved

weight how many pounds you weigh. Licenses often require height, weight, and hair and eye color for identification.

Example

MOTOR VEHICLE SERVICES APPLICATION FOR DRIVER LICENSE
PLEASE COMPLETE BOTH SIDES - PRINT CLEARLY
DRIVER LICENSE NUMBER

CHECK APPROPRIATE
BOXES BELOW

Jesse   J   Grabow

FIRST NAME   M   LAST NAME

NON PHOTO
PHOTO   X

Jul 4, 19--   M   BLUE   150   5'7"   036 44 5566

DATE OF BIRTH (MO, DAY YEAR)   SEX   EYE COLOR   WT   HEIGHT   SOCIAL SECURITY NUMBER

146 MAPLE DRIVE

INITIAL   X
RENEWAL
DUPLICATE
CHANGE

MAILING ADDRESS (STREET, PO BOX, RURAL ROUTE)   STREET ADDRESS (IF DIFFERENT FROM MAILING ADDRESS)

Lafayette   CA   97321   Marin

CITY   STATE   ZIP   COUNTY   CITY   STATE   ZIP   COUNTY

1. Do you have a valid   YES   2. Is your driving privilege   YES   3. Do you suffer from any   YES
driver license in any   <u>NO</u>   now suspended in any   <u>NO</u>   mental, physical or   <u>NO</u>
other state?   state?   convulsive disorder?

4. Are you in this country legally?   <u>YES</u>
     NO

Jesse Grabow   Aug. 9. 19---

--DATE----------------------------

X SIGN HERE. I, THE APPLICANT, CERTIFY THE STATEMENTS ON BOTH SIDES OF THIS APPLICATION ARE CORRECT

If you answered "yes" to questions 1, 2, or 3, you must explain your answer on the back of the card.

IF YOU ANSWERED YES TO QUESTIONS 1, 2, OR 3, PLEASE EXPLAIN:

Procedure ▼

Be sure you have all the documents you need with you and that you follow the directions very carefully. Read the entire application first. Don't be afraid to ask questions if there's something you don't understand.

Print clearly, using a pen. Be sure you answer all questions truthfully. Many people choose to have a photo license because it is a good form of identification. In some states, a photo ID is required.

After you fill out the application, read it again carefully to make sure you have answered all the questions and checked the boxes you meant to check. Your signature should be your name the way you write it all the time, not printed the way you did at the top of the application.

Practice ▼

Now it's your turn.

Task: to apply for a driver's license

Situation: Congratulations! You have passed your road test, your eye test and your written test. Now you are ready to apply for your driver's license. Fill out the form on page 52. Remember, if you answer "yes" to questions 1, 2, or 3, you must explain your answer on the back of the card.

MOTOR VEHICLE SERVICES APPLICATION FOR DRIVER LICENSE
PLEASE COMPLETE BOTH SIDES - PRINT CLEARLY
DRIVER LICENSE NUMBER

CHECK APPROPRIATE
BOXES BELOW

FIRST NAME   M   LAST NAME

NON PHOTO

PHOTO

DATE OF BIRTH (MO, DAY YEAR)   SEX   EYE COLOR   WT   HEIGHT   SOCIAL SECURITY NUMBER

INITIAL

RENEWAL   MAILING ADDRESS (STREET, PO BOX, RURAL ROUTE)   STREET ADDRESS (IF DIFFERENT FROM MAILING ADDRESS)

DUPLICATE

CHANGE

CITY   STATE   ZIP   COUNTY   CITY   STATE   ZIP   COUNTY

----

1. Do you have a valid   YES   2. Is your driving privilege   YES   3. Do you suffer from any   YES
   driver license in any   NO   now suspended in any   NO   mental, physical or   NO
   other state?   state?   convulsive disorder?

4. Are you in this country legally?   YES
                                          NO

--DATE----------------------------

X SIGN HERE. I, THE APPLICANT, CERTIFY THE STATEMENTS ON BOTH SIDES OF THIS APPLICATION ARE CORRECT

IF YOU ANSWERED YES TO QUESTIONS 1, 2, OR 3, PLEASE EXPLAIN:

Applying for a Library Card

A public library allows us to borrow books, magazines, videos, CDs, and cassettes for a certain period of time, usually two weeks, without any charge. Owning a library card is one of the least expensive ways to keep informed and/or entertained. It's usually very easy to get a library card in the town or city where you live. Bring identification with you that shows who you are and that you do live in the town. If your town has no library, you can often get a library card in a neighboring town or in the city where you work. Many states have reciprocal agreements where people can use their card from one library to borrow materials from other libraries in the county where they live. There is not one rule for all towns or all libraries, but the librarian in each will help you apply for a card.

Rationale

The library is a great place to read newspapers and magazines in peace and quiet, without having to buy any. It's often a meeting place for book clubs, where people get together to discuss the latest books. Best of all, it's a place where, free of charge, you can read, either there or anywhere you choose, the latest novels and nonfiction; you can research a special interest or hobby or a homework assignment; you can explore the countless opportunities to enjoy one of America's greatest free resources. You can also find the library is not free if you don't return your books, videos, etc., on time (the due date is stamped on a card so you'll know when it should be returned). The fine is small at most libraries, but it can add up. There is nothing easier to fill out than an application for a library card. Remember to bring identification with you.

Materials Needed

pen, identification (picture ID is best) showing name, address, and age, if you are under 18; a utility bill (gas, electric, telephone) or lease showing place of residence

Skills Involved

reading; writing simple English; following directions

Important Vocabulary

apply ask for, usually in writing

book discussion group a group of people meeting to talk about a book they've all read

borrow keep for a certain amount of time. To borrow something means to return it at a later date.

county a geographic area in a state for governing purposes, usually a group of neighboring cities and towns

countless too many to count; a very large amount

damages damages to books include tears, stains, making marks on the pages

due date the day a book, video, etc., should be returned to the library

fine money paid if material is damaged or returned late to the library (after the due date)

free of charge without paying anything

hobby something you like to do in your free time

identification abbreviated id, proof of who you are; for example, your passport or birth certificate

lease a paper signed by the landlord and tenant (owner and person renting a house or apartment) that tells how long the tenant can live there, how much the rent is, and other information

least expensive cheap; costing very little money

neighboring town town or city near the one you live in

nonfiction true stories, facts, events

novels fiction; make-believe stories

prompt on time

public library free library open to everyone

reciprocal sharing; helping supply each other with books and materials, for example

research to look for material on a particular subject

residence place where you live

resources places to get information needed

signature your name as you write it by hand

utility bill a paper showing how much money is owed for using a particular utility: gas, electric, telephone, etc. Most people get a utility bill at the place where they live.

Example

```
NAME Shanti                              Ramkumar
            first          middle        last
ADDRESS 144 Plaza Rd                              include apartment number

CITY FairLawn                            NJ  07410
                              I apply for the right to use the library and promise
PHONE 201 794 0000               to obey all its rules, to take good care of all books
                                   I borrow, to pay all fines or damages charged to me
                                   and to give prompt notice of change in my address.
OTHER                         SIGNATURE
                                Shanti  Ramkumar
```

Procedure ▼

Bring your identification to the library. Be sure the information you write on the card is the same as what's on your ID (identification). Ask questions if you don't understand something. The librarian is there to help you.

Practice ▼

Now it's your turn.

Task: to apply for a library card

Situation: You have moved to a new town and want to be able to use the library. Fill out the application below. Remember to have your identification in front of you.

```
NAME  --------------------------------------------------------------------
            FIRST              MIDDLE              LAST

ADDRESS  ---------------------------------------------------------------

CITY  ------------------------------------- STATE --------- ZIP  -----------
                                              I apply for the right to use the library and
promise
PHONE                                      to obey all its rules, to take good care of all books
                                              I borrow, to pay all fines or damages charged to me
                                              and to give prompt notice of change in my address.

OTHER  -------------------------        SIGNATURE
                                        -------------------------------------
```

Look at the card.

- Did you write your name as it appears on your ID?

- Did you include important information such as your apartment number if you live in an apartment building?

Check your card carefully.

Now take your ID, go to your nearest public library and apply for a card. Welcome to the wonderful world of free entertainment and education.

Unit Three

Letters and Mail Orders

Ordering Tickets Through the Mail

You're planning a vacation in New York City next month. While you're there, you would like to see a Broadway show or a ballet at Lincoln Center. Since you know when you'd like to go to the theater and how much money you want to spend, writing a letter with a check or money order enclosed is a good way to get the tickets of your choice.

Rationale

There are several ways to get tickets for a show, concert, sporting event, or other performance. You can

- call on the telephone and give a credit card number,

- go to the theater or arena where the event will take place, or

- write for tickets.

If you call on the telephone, you have the advantage of knowing immediately if and when tickets are available. The disadvantages are that you don't always know where your seats will be, you must have a credit card to pay for the tickets, and you must pay a service charge for each ticket.

If you live near the theater or arena, you can go right to the box office to buy your tickets. The advantages to this method are that you will know immediately what seats are available on what dates. You also have the choice of paying by cash, credit card, or check. The disadvantages to this method are that the box office may not be open when you are free to go there, and you may not live or work in the area.

The third alternative is to write a letter of request. The disadvantages to this approach are that you have to wait to hear if the seats you want are available at the times you requested, and you can't use cash or credit cards. Naturally, the more time you give the theater to fill your request, the better chance you have of receiving the tickets you want.

Materials Needed

unlined stationery or typing paper, two envelopes, pen or typewriter, check or money order, postage stamps

Skills Involved

writing a check or purchasing a money order; organizing thoughts; giving specific details; using correct spelling, punctuation, and capitalization

Important Vocabulary

arena an area used for sports or other entertainment, usually enclosed in a building

balcony an upper level containing seats in a theater

box office a place where you can buy tickets for a show or other events

closing a word or phrase used to end a letter. The closing is found just above the writer's signature and is always followed by a comma.

concert a performance or show given by one or more musicians

Enc. abbreviation for *enclosure*, written at the end of a letter when you include items other than the letter in the envelope

matinee an afternoon performance

mezzanine a lower balcony in a theater (sometimes the first few rows of seats in a lower balcony)

money order a kind of check purchased from a bank or post office for a specific amount of money, often used for sending a payment through the mail

return address the address of the person sending a note or letter

self-addressed, stamped envelope an envelope that you address to yourself with the correct postage on it. You enclose this envelope with your letter of request so the tickets you ask for can be mailed to you as quickly as possible. You will often see this abbreviated *SASE*.

service charge an extra charge that is added to the price of tickets when you order them by telephone

Example

103 Smith St.
Minneapolis, MN 55403
Nov. 24, 19—

Box Office
New York City Ballet
New York State Theater
Lincoln Center
New York, NY 10023

Enclosed are a self-addressed, stamped envelope and a check for eighty dollars ($80.00). Please send me two (2) tickets for the best possible seats, center mezzanine, for The Nutcracker ballet for Monday evening, December 25; Tuesday evening, December 26; or Wednesday matinee, December 27. Location is important, but I will be in New York for those dates only, so I would appreciate the best possible seats you can give me for one of those three dates. Thank You.

Sincerely,

Phutak Chong
Phutak Chong

Enc.

Procedure A: Writing the Letter ▼

1.   Use unlined paper and be sure to write clearly in ink (or use a typewriter or word processor). You can use small stationery as long as there is enough room in the envelope for the letter, a check or money order, and a return envelope.

2.   Put your return address and the date in the upper right-hand corner.

14 Beverly Dr. 9C
Los Angeles, CA 90024
June 1, 19—

3.   Leave a blank space below the date. Then, on the left side of the paper, write the address as it will appear on the envelope.

<u>Phantom of the Opera</u>
P.O. Box 993
Times Square Station
New York, NY 10108

4.   Leave a blank space and then write your message. Explain what you are including in the envelope and describe the specific tickets you want. Be sure to tell

   •   the date or dates you want the tickets for,
   •   the number of tickets you want, and
   •   where you would prefer to sit.

   If you give more than one date, you might want to tell which is your first choice. If you give only one specific date, you may wish to ask for "the best possible seats" rather than specifying a particular location, especially if the play, ballet, or concert is very popular. At the end of your message, it's always nice to say "thank you."

Enclosed are a self-addressed, stamped envelope and a money order for sixty dollars ($60.00). Please send two (2) tickets, preferably center mezzanine, for Wednesday, July 5, for <u>Phantom of the Opera</u>. Since that is the only time I will be in New York, I would appreciate the best seats possible for that date. Thank you.

5.   Leave a blank space, then put your closing on the right side of the paper and sign your complete name under it. If you are typing your letter, leave enough space between the closing and your typed name to sign your name in ink.

6.   Below your name, on the left, put *Enc.* to indicate that you are enclosing other items in the envelope.

Sincerely,

Ludmila Tcheroff

Ludmila Tcheroff

Enc.

7. Address an envelope to yourself and put on the correct postage.

Ms. Ludmila Tcheroff
14 Beverly Dr., 9C
Los Angeles, CA 90024

8. If you are enclosing a check, make it out to the name of the show. On the bottom of the check, write what it is for so that if it should get separated from your letter, it will be easy to identify. A money order should have the same information written on it.

9. Put the check inside your letter and put them in an envelope with the self-addressed envelope. Be sure all the necessary items are enclosed.

Practice A ▼

Now it's your turn.

Task: to order tickets for a concert

Situation: Your favorite musical group is coming to a theater in a city near you next month. They will be performing there for one week. You want to order tickets for you and a friend for a Saturday evening or Sunday matinee performance. Be sure to enclose a self-addressed, stamped envelope and a check or money order.

Procedure B: Addressing the Envelope ▼

1. Put your name and address (the *return address*) in the upper left-hand corner of the envelope so that if the letter cannot be delivered for some reason, it will be returned to you.

2. In the center of the envelope, write or type the address of the theater or box office exactly as it appears on your letter.

3. Put a postage stamp in the upper right-hand corner. Be sure to use the right amount of postage, or the letter will not be delivered.

Your finished envelope should look something like this:

Ms. Ludmila Tcheroff
14 Beverly Dr. 9C
Los Angeles, CA 90024

Phantom of the Opera
P.O. Box 993
Times Square Station
New York, NY 10108

Practice B ▼

Now it's your turn.

Task: to address the envelope

Situation: You have written a letter requesting tickets to a concert. Now you want to mail it.

Procedure C: Folding the Letter ▼

See page 21 for the instructions and diagrams on how to fold a letter.

Practice C ▼

Now it's your turn.

Task: to fold your letter properly

Situation: You have proofread your letter, and now you want to send it. Fold your letter and put it in the envelope.

Hope you get good seats!

10 Writing a Letter of Complaint

In this age of computers and machines, it's very hard to find a person to talk to when you find an error on a bill or on an order for merchandise bought through the mail. In most companies, everything seems to be handled by machines—everything, that is, except correcting errors.

Rationale

If you find a mistake on a bill, you can call the company and try to have it corrected, but there can be many problems with this approach.

You have nothing in writing to prove that you have notified the company of the error.

The person you speak to may not be qualified to correct the error or may forget to take care of it and later deny any knowledge of it.

You may end up having to pay interest on the unpaid bill until the error is corrected, and worse, you may spoil your good credit rating.

If you write a letter of complaint and keep a copy of it, you have proof that you have notified the company about the error. In the letter, you can explain exactly what is wrong so that the problem will be directed to the right person, and all the information is there in writing for the person to check so he or she doesn't have to try to remember what you said. If you have any receipts, you can send *copies* of them along to prove your points. (You'll want to save the original bills and receipts for yourself.)

Materials Needed

practice paper, unlined stationery, envelope, pen (or typewriter), bill, receipts, correct mailing address, access to a copying machine or carbon paper, postage stamp

Skills Involved

using correct spelling, punctuation, and capitalization; using correct letter form; supplying specific details in organized paragraphs

Important Vocabulary

bill a piece of paper that tells how much money you owe someone for merchandise you bought or for services (such as the telephone or electricity) you used

closing a word or phrase used to end a letter. The closing is found just above the writer's signature and is always followed by a comma.

complaint an expression of unhappiness or dissatisfaction about something

credit rating information about how you pay your bills. If you charge items to credit cards and fail to pay your bills, you will get a bad credit rating. This information is available to other companies and might make it difficult for you to charge things or obtain loans in the future.

enclosed inside. If you have enclosed something in a letter, it means you have put it in the envelope with the letter. The abbreviation *Enc.* at the end of a business letter tells the reader to look for other items in the envelope.

interest extra money charged if bills aren't paid on time

merchandise items for sale

notified told in writing

re: about; with regard to. Often used at the beginning of a business letter to indicate the subject of the letter.

receipt a written statement showing that you have received certain merchandise or have paid a certain amount of money

return address the address of the person sending something in the mail.

salutation the greeting in a letter, usually beginning with *Dear* followed by a person's name

shipping and handling charges the cost of shipping (mailing) and handling (assembling and preparing for mailing) your order. When you order merchandise through the mail, you are often charged for these.

To whom it may concern a salutation used when you don't know the name or the title of the person you should write to

Example

> 157 Ridge Ave.
> Seattle, WA 98110
> April 14, 19—
>
> Rick Rabbit Emporium
> P.O. Box 5555
> Portland, OR 97223
>
> Re: Order # 85942
>
> To whom it may concern:
>
> On March 1, I ordered 3 pink rabbits at $9.95 each and 3 flower baskets at $11.95 each for a total of $65.70 plus shipping and handling, $11.50. This brings the final total to $77.20.
>
> Enclosed is a copy of your receipt, which came with my order. Today I received a bill for $87.15 for 4 pink rabbits and 3 flower baskets. Since I didn't order 4 rabbits and I never received 4 rabbits, I'm enclosing a check for the original amount, $77.20, for the merchandise I did receive. Please correct your billing. Thank you.
>
> Sincerely,
>
> Prunella Pasquale
>
> Enc

problem is stated here

Procedure A: Writing the Letter ▼

1. Write a practice copy first so you can proofread it and correct any mistakes or add anything you may have left out the first time.

2. On unlined stationery, put your return address and the date in the upper right-hand corner. This information is extremely important for easy identification, so an answer can be mailed to you.

157 Ridge Ave.
Seattle, WA 98110
April 14, 19

3. Leave a blank space below the date. Then, on the left, write the name and address of the company that sent you the incorrect bill.

Rick Rabbit Emporium
P.O. Box 5555
Portland, OR 97223

4. If you have an account number or any kind of order number, leave a blank space and write it below the company's address. This information makes it easier for the person who receives your letter to check into the problem.

Re: Order # 85942

5.   Leave a blank space and then write the salutation. If you don't know the name or title of a particular person to write to, write:

To whom it may concern:

This will get your letter directed to the right person.

6.   Leave a blank space below the salutation and write your message. Be very specific. Tell exactly what the problem is. If you have been charged for merchandise you never ordered or for merchandise you ordered but never received, say so. Tell exactly what merchandise you're talking about and give the price.

If you have been charged an incorrect amount, tell what the correct amount should be and enclose *copies* of any receipts or proof you might have. Don't send originals. They are all the proof you have.

7.   Leave a blank space below your message and put your closing on the right. *Sincerely* is a good word to use for the closing. Sign your complete name under your closing. If you type your letter, leave enough space between the closing and your typed name to sign your name in ink.

Sincerely,

Prunella Pasquale

Prunella Pasquale

8.   Below your name, on the left, put *Enc.* to indicate that you have enclosed other items in the envelope.

9.   Make a copy of your letter to keep for yourself. At the same time, make copies of the bill and any receipts you want to send with the letter. Keep the originals.

Practice A ▼

Now it's your turn.

Task: to write a letter of complaint

Situation: You have received a bill from ABC Shirt and Pants Mail Order, PO Box 2143, Garden City, NY 11535, for two shirts and two pairs of pants you ordered through the mail. You ordered two shirts, size medium, on sale at $17.95 each, and two pairs of pants, size large, at $27.50 a pair. Shipping and handling charges were $9.95. You were billed for two shirts at the regular price of $20.95. The other charges were correct. Your order number was 1432648. Write a letter to the company explaining the problem.

Read your letter over again and ask yourself these questions:

Did you tell exactly what you ordered and how much each item cost?

Did you remember to add up the amount you should have been charged?

Procedure B: Addressing the Envelope ▼

The name and address of the company you're writing to should be written or typed the same way inside the letter and on the envelope.

1. Put your name and address (the *return address*) in the upper left-hand corner of the envelope so that if the letter cannot be delivered for some reason, it will be returned to you.

2. In the center of the envelope, write or type the name and address of the company you have written to. Put the name of the company on the first line, the street name and number (or PO box number) on the next line, and the city, state, and zip code on a third line. If the letter is going outside the country you are writing from, be sure to put the name of the country on a fourth line.

3. Put a postage stamp in the upper right-hand corner. Be sure to use the right amount of postage, or the letter will not be delivered.

Your finished envelope should look something like this:

Prunella Pasquale
157 Ridge Ave.
Seattle, WA 98110

Rick Rabbit Emporium
P. O. Box 5555
Portland, OR 97223

Practice B ▼

Now it's your turn.

Task: to address the envelope

Situation: You have written a letter of complaint. Now you want to mail it.

Procedure C: Folding the Letter ▼

See page 21 for the instructions and diagrams on how to fold a letter.

Practice C ▼

Now it's your turn.

Task: to fold your letter properly

Situation: You have proofread your letter, and now you want to send it. Fold your letter and put it in the envelope.

Correcting an Error on Your Credit Card Bill

On the back of every credit card statement, there is a very important section telling you what to do in case of errors or questions about your bill. The laws of the United States (federal law) require this statement. You cannot just call a credit card company and complain. You must put it in writing. Every statement says:

> In Case of Errors or Questions About Your Bill: If you think your bill is wrong, or if you need more information about a transaction on your bill, write us on a separate sheet at the address for billing inquiries shown on the front of this statement as soon as possible. We must hear from you no later than 60 days after we sent you the first bill on which the error or problem appeared. You can telephone us, but doing so will not preserve your rights.
>
> In your letter, give us the following information:
>
> - Your name and account number
>
> - The dollar amount of the suspected error
>
> - Describe the error, and explain, if you can, why you believe it is an error. If you need more information, describe the item you are unsure about.
>
> You do not have to pay any amount in question while we are investigating, but you are still obligated to pay the parts of your bill that are not in question. While we investigate your question, we cannot report you as delinquent or take any action to collect the amount you question.

What this is saying is that you have the right within 60 days of receiving your bill to write and question it, providing the information asked for. They will not charge you or add interest on that item while it is in dispute.

Rationale

Credit cards are easy to get and easier to get in trouble with. If you have a credit card, you must check it carefully each month to be sure it is correct. The credit card company pays your bill and then sends it to you. Only you will recognize an error, so you are responsible for writing as soon as possible to tell the company about a charge that doesn't belong on your card, a mistake in the price of an item, an item that was never received, etc. Be sure you keep a copy of all your charge receipts (the paper you sign when you charge something) and make a copy of your letter and any other items you are sending to the credit card company and keep them in a folder or other safe place.

Materials Needed

copy of bill, copy of receipt for disputed item, information requested in "About your bill," stationery, pen or typewriter/word processor, address where information is to be sent

Skills Involved

organizing and presenting specific information; typing or word processing; using correct spelling, punctuation, capitalization, and letter form

Important Vocabulary

complain say something is wrong

delinquent late

errors mistakes

in dispute being questioned

investigating checking the item in dispute

obligated to pay must pay

suspected error you think it is a mistake

transaction purchase you are being asked to pay for

Example

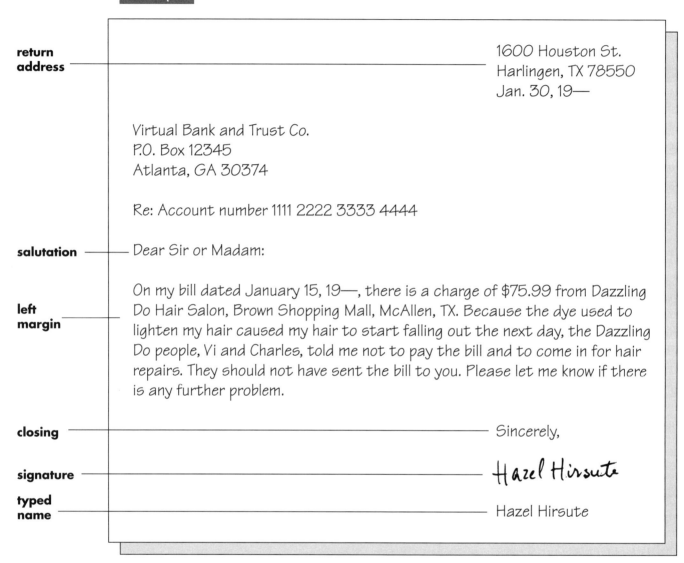

return
address

1600 Houston St.
Harlingen, TX 78550
Jan. 30, 19—

Virtual Bank and Trust Co.
P.O. Box 12345
Atlanta, GA 30374

Re: Account number 1111 2222 3333 4444

salutation — Dear Sir or Madam:

left
margin

On my bill dated January 15, 19—, there is a charge of $75.99 from Dazzling
Do Hair Salon, Brown Shopping Mall, McAllen, TX. Because the dye used to
lighten my hair caused my hair to start falling out the next day, the Dazzling
Do people, Vi and Charles, told me not to pay the bill and to come in for hair
repairs. They should not have sent the bill to you. Please let me know if there
is any further problem.

closing

Sincerely,

signature

Hazel Hirsute

typed
name

Hazel Hirsute

Procedure A: Writing the Letter ▼

1.   Write a practice copy first so you can proofread it and correct any mistakes. Be sure
to check that you have included all the information asked for.

2.   On unlined stationery, put your return address and the date in the upper right-hand
corner. This information is extremely important for easy identification and so a reply
can be mailed to you.

1600 Houston St.
Harlingen, TX 78550
Jan. 30, 19—

3. Leave a blank space below the date. Then, on the left, write the name and address of the company that sent you the bill.

Virtual Bank and Trust Co.
P.O. Box 12345
Atlanta, GA 30374

4. Leave a blank space and on the left write the number of your credit card. This is extremely important if you want a fast response. *Re:* in front of the number means "this is about...". You can also include the date the card expires (will no longer be good).

Re: Account number 1111 2222 3333 4444

5. Leave a blank space and then write the salutation and the name(s) of the person(s) you are writing to. If you don't have the name of a particular person to write to, you can write:

Dear Sir or Madam:

or

To Whom It May Concern:

This will get your letter directed to the right person.

6.   Leave a blank space below the salutation and write your message. Be very specific. Give the date of the transaction, the amount shown on the bill, and tell exactly what the problem is—if it is a mistake in price, if you never received the merchandise you were charged for, if you were not supposed to be charged for the item and the reason why.

On my bill dated January 15, 19—, there is a charge of $75.99 from Dazzling Do Hair Salon, Brown Shopping Mall, McAllen, TX. Because the dye used to lighten my hair caused my hair to start falling out the next day, the Dazzling Do people, Vi and Charles, told me not to pay the bill and to come in for hair repairs. They should not have sent the bill to you. Please let me know if there is any further problem.

Besides all the information asked for on the back of the bill, be sure to also include copies of any receipts, documentation (proof), letters, etc., to prove your point. Remember to make copies of any papers and receipts to send. These documents are all the proof you have. If you have nothing in writing to prove your claim, include the name(s), address(es), and/or telephone number(s) of anyone who can verify your claim (who can tell the billing company you are telling the truth.)

7.   Leave a blank space below your message and put your closing on the right. *Sincerely* is a good word to use for the closing. Sign your complete name under your closing. If you type your letter, leave enough space between the closing and your typed name to sign your name in ink.

Sincerely,

Hazel Hirsute

Hazel Hirsute

8.   Below your name, on the left, put *Enc.* (an abbreviation for *enclosure*) to indicate that you have enclosed other items in the envelope.

Enc.

9.   Make a copy of your letter to keep for yourself. Be sure to keep it with copies of the bill and any receipts you are sending to the company.

Practice A ▼

Now it's your turn.

Task: to write a letter questioning a charge on your credit card statement

Situation: Your credit card statement shows you owe $74.96 for books you bought at the Red Eye bookstore. You returned two of the books to the store the next day and received a credit of $32, which does not appear on your statement. All the other charges on your statement were correct. Write a letter to the credit card company explaining the problem.

Read your letter over again. Ask yourself these questions:

*   Did you tell exactly what the problem was, including when you returned the items and how much they cost?

*   Did you attach a copy of the sales receipt and the credit receipt?

*   Did you make copies of everything for your file?

Procedure B: Addressing the Envelope ▼

The name and address of the company you're writing to should be written or typed the same way inside the letter and on the envelope.

1. Put your name and address (*the return address*) in the upper left-hand corner of the envelope so that if the letter cannot be delivered for some reason, it will be returned to you.

2. In the center of the envelope, write or type the name and address of the company you have written to. Put the name of the company on the first line, the street name and number (or PO box number) on the next line, and the city, state, and zip code on a third line. If the letter is going outside the country you are writing from, be sure to put the name of the country on a fourth line.

3. Put a postage stamp in the upper right-hand corner. Be sure to use the right amount of postage or the letter will not be delivered.

Your finished envelope should look something like this:

Ms. Hazel Hirsute
1600 Houston St.
Harlingen, TX 78550

Virtual Bank and Trust Co.
P.O. Box 12345
Atlanta, GA 30374

Practice B ▼

Now it's your turn.

Task: to address the envelope

Situation: You have written a letter to the credit card company advising them of an error on your bill. Now you want to mail the letter.

Procedure C: Folding the Letter ▼

See page 21 for the instructions and diagrams on how to fold a letter.

Practice C ▼

Now it's your turn.

Task: to fold your letter properly

Situation: You have proofread your letter, and now you want to send it. Fold your letter and put it in the envelope.

Unit Four

Beginning
Academic
Writing

Using a Graphic Organizer

There are many ways to organize our thoughts. A really easy way is to create a graphic organizer. Just as its name suggests, it is a way of organizing our thoughts on paper. There are outlines (see Book 2 of this set, *Practical English Writing Skills*, Chapter 9), Venn diagrams, and webs, for example.

Rationale

You have to write an essay for class and you don't know what to include. You know what you want to write about, but there are so many thoughts going around in your mind, you don't know where to begin or how to put your thoughts together so they make sense. An easy way to do it is to write down your main topic and work from there.

Materials Needed

pen or pencil, paper, ruler, compass or something to help you make circles (optional), colored pens or pencils (optional), notes on the subject (optional)

Skills Involved

organizing thoughts; using graphics

Important Vocabulary

appointed chosen for a job

autobiography a person's story of one's own life

carbohydrates sugars, starches that give energy to the body

compass a V-shaped instrument used for drawing circles

components parts of a whole

create make

diagram a drawing to explain an idea

diet food and drink

elected chosen by people's vote; not appointed

essay a short piece of writing on a subject

executive the chief person in charge of governing

graphic written signs or drawings

judicial the part of the system that judges (decides) what is legal

legislative the branch of government that makes the laws

notes information collected to use for an essay, outline, etc.

optional voluntary, not necessary

serve to work in a position

term the length of time a person serves

topic (subject) thing you want to talk or write about

trigger set off, start

Venn diagram a group of circles related to a central topic but not necessarily to each other. Things that are related to a central circle overlap that circle but not each other. See Example.

web a net of thin threads tying something together; a network

With a Venn diagram, you can put your main topic in a circle in the center of a page and then draw circles to show how things are related and connected. For example, if your topic is "A Healthy Diet", you would write *Healthy Diet* in a circle, then draw circles around the center, connecting each circle only with the center to show what goes into making a healthy diet.

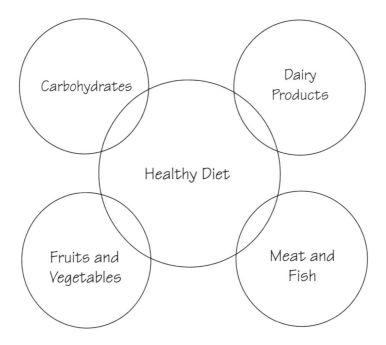

These are some of the things the writer feels are important in a healthy diet. Can you think of more? Add your circles to the group. Notice that each circle is complete by itself, but is connected to the main circle, *Healthy Diet*. More circles can be added around each: for example, *apples, bananas, potatoes* could be connecting circles to *fruits and vegetables*. Each circle will trigger more information in your brain, so that when you are finished, you will be ready to write an organized essay, discussing not only the components of a healthy diet, but also giving examples of each component.

Example

A *web* is another way to organize your thoughts. If you are going to write a paper about the organization of the United States government, for example, you might start with an inner circle and create a web as your ideas spin from the central idea. You can use different-colored pens or pencils to identify each part of your web.

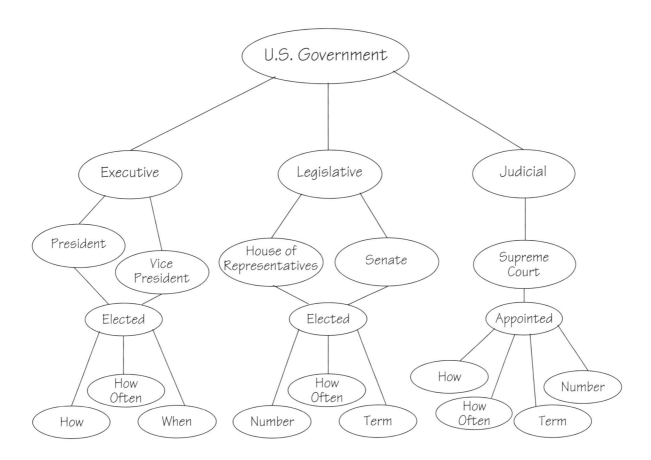

From this web and your information, you would be able to write an essay about the United States government and the fact that it is divided into three branches: executive, legislative, and judicial. You can explain who is elected and who is appointed, how long people serve, and anything else you wish to add. By looking at your web, you will know not only what information you want to include, but also how to organize it so it is easy to read and understand.

Procedure ▼

1.   Decide what your main topic will be and put it in a circle in the center of your page. Don't worry about making perfect lines.

2.   Think about what makes a healthy diet. Look at the information you have collected. Make an organizer of the kinds of foods you think people need.

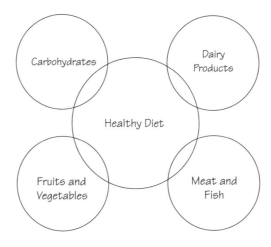

3.   Add examples to each part of the organizer.

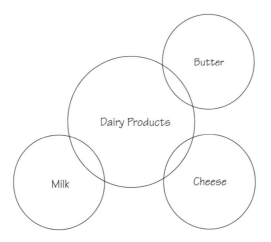

4. Add anything else you want to include in your organizer.

5. Do this for each circle until you have included all the ideas you can think of for your essay. Your finished organizer might look like this.

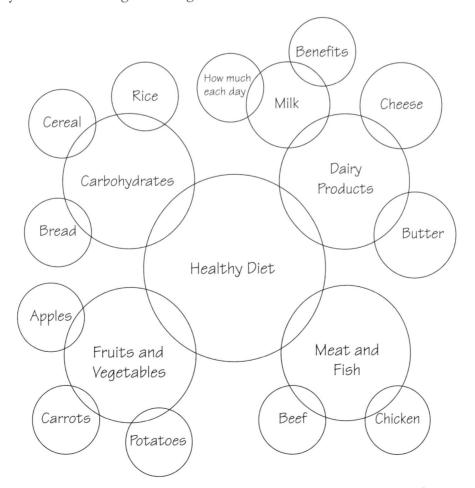

Practice ▼

Now it's your turn.

Task: to create a web for an autobiography

Situation: You need to write an autobiography for your guidance counselor, who will help you plan for your future. You want to tell something about your childhood, your favorite subjects, your hobbies, and your plans for the future. Organize your thoughts with a web. You can use MY LIFE as your central circle. When you finish your organizer, look at it again. Can you write an organized essay from it?

13

Writing a Lab Report

Just about everyone who goes through an academic program at the high school and/or university level has to write a lab report at one time or another. Writing reports is something we get to do through most of our lives. We don't always think of it as writing a report, but there we are filling out forms telling why we're doing it, what prompted the report, the results, etc. The more organized our information, the easier it is to write about and to have others understand, whether it's for a science class or a police accident report for our insurance company.

Rationale

Knowing how to write a lab report has lots of benefits:

- better grades in science classes where they're required,

- seeing for yourself if you really understand what has happened during the lab, and

- improving your organizational skills, which will carry over into your life in and out of school.

Materials Needed

lab report forms (if applicable) or paper to complete the report, pen or word-processing equipment, materials involved in the particular experiment being conducted (done)

Skills Involved

comprehension; following directions; observing; collecting and organizing information; spelling, punctuation, good grammar

Important Vocabulary

academic subjects such as *languages, science,* and *math* are academic subjects

apparatus items needed for an experiment

experiment a test to see how something will turn out (end)

forceps or tweezers a tool used for picking up, holding, or pulling things

lab short for laboratory, a place where experiments take place

prompted caused. A new illness might prompt experiments to find a cure.

report written information stating *purpose* (why you're doing the experiment), *procedure* (step-by-step description of activities to be done), *observations* (writing down what happens during the experiment as it is taking place), *conclusion*, which should tell you whether your purpose was accomplished. Your *conclusion* would include specific information proving your point.

sparker a lighter used instead of matches

Note: Different lab reports may use different vocabulary (words) about the experiment you are working on.

Example

Laboratory Report

The Bunsen Burner

Purpose: To learn how the Bunsen burner works because it is a source of heat in the laboratory.

Apparatus and Materials

heat-resistant mat, burner and tubing, evaporating dish, forceps or tweezers, sparker, 18-gauge copper wire (see illustration)

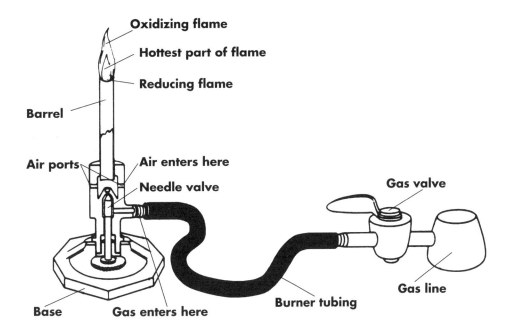

Procedures

Note: Make sure you are protected before working with the burner. You should be wearing safety goggles (glasses), an apron and gloves. You should not have long sleeves or loose jewelry or clothing, and your hair should be away from your face and tied back if it is long.

1. Know something about the construction of your burner.

    a. It should have a gas inlet in the base (where the gas enters), a vertical tube (barrel) where the gas is mixed with air, and adjustable openings (ports) in the base of the barrel. These ports admit air to the gas stream.

    b. There may be an adjustable needle valve to regulate the flow of gas, or it may be regulated by adjusting the gas valve on the supply line.

    c. The burner is always turned off at the gas valve, never at the needle valve.

2. a. Partially close the ports at the base of the tube.

    b. Turn the gas on full.

    c. Hold the sparker about 5 cm above the top of the burner and light it.

    d. Adjust the gas flow until the flame has the desired height. If you need a very low flame, ports should be partially closed when the gas pressure is reduced so the flame doesn't burn inside the base of the tube. This could make the barrel get very hot, and the flame can produce carbon monoxide, which is a poisonous gas!

If the flame is burning inside the base of the barrel, turn off the gas at the gas valve immediately. Don't touch the barrel of the burner or you'll get burned. Let the barrel cool off and then:

e. Partially close the ports to decrease the amount of air admitted to the burner.

f. Turn the gas on full, and re-light the burner. Remember to control the height of the flame by adjusting the gas valve.

3. When the flame is burning safely and steadily, experiment by completely closing the ports at the base of the burner. What is the result?

   Answer: Flame turns orange and flickers.

4. Using forceps or tweezers, hold an evaporating dish in the tip of the flame for about 3 minutes. Place the dish on a heat-resistant mat and allow it to cool. Then turn it over and look at the bottom. Describe the results and suggest a possible explanation.

   Answer: The dish turns black because of carbon deposits from the orange flame.

5. It is important to adjust the flame so it is free of the orange color and the "roaring" sound that happens when there is too much air admitted. What is your conclusion?

   Conclusion: Oxygen is needed to completely burn all the carbon in the gas.

Procedure ▼

1. Read all the directions for the experiment first. Be sure you understand what to do. Follow all the safety precautions carefully. This is very important.

2. Get all your equipment ready.

3. On a note pad or paper, write the purpose of your experiment.

   Purpose: To discover the influence of smell on taste and texture.

4. Next, write the Procedure you're following step by step:

   Line up samples of cake, garlic, spiced meat, orange juice, and chocolate.

   Taste each one, rinsing your mouth carefully between tastes so they are not mixed.

   Write down how each item tastes: sweet, spicy, etc.

Shut off breathing passages by holding the nose so nothing can be smelled. Taste each item again, again rinsing your mouth between tastes.

5. As you do the experiment, write down your observations.

    Observation: The items don't change in color or texture, yet everything seems tasteless.

6. From what you have observed, come to a conclusion.

    Conclusion: Our sense of taste is governed by our sense of smell, which is probably why people who have a cold and stuffed nose don't enjoy their food as much as when they are healthy.

Practice ▼

Now it's your turn.

Task: to write a lab report

Situation: You want to see which food products contain starch, a white, solid, tasteless carbohydrate found in many foods. Your teacher will present an experiment using a small bottle of iodine and a selection of fruits, vegetables, and other foods. Observe the experiment and use your own paper to write the report.

Writing a Descriptive Paragraph

We are often influenced by other people's descriptions: of their vacations, of their homeland, their new boyfriend or girlfriend, a television program or movie, etc. Being able to describe something so others can see it through our words is not an easy task. We have to be able to organize our thoughts enough so our description is not a jumble of words—so people can actually visualize what we're talking about.

Rationale

Organizing our thoughts so others understand them is important in our social, academic, and professional lives. Whether we're explaining what it was like to live in a certain country or the effects of acid rain on the environment; whether we're describing the funniest experience we've ever had or writing about our backgrounds for a college or business application, we need to put our facts in logical order.

Materials Needed

word processor, typewriter or pen/pencil and paper; graphic organizer or outline to organize our thoughts; information/facts for description

Skills Involved

organizing thoughts; focusing on a topic sentence; writing a coherent paragraph with specific information in logical order; using correct spelling, punctuation, and grammar

Important Vocabulary

appointed chosen by someone for a certain job

approves says it's okay

autobiography/biodata piece of writing about yourself

bill a plan for a law

branches sections, parts of a whole

checks and balances a system of government that protects citizens from unfair practices by any one branch of government. Each branch watches over the others to ensure that no one group gets special treatment.

coherent makes sense, understandable

confirmed agreed to appoint someone to a position

Constitution the Supreme Law of the United States

dependent having to rely on someone/something else; opposite of *independent*

elected chosen by vote

focus see a true, clear picture of something

graphic organizer see Chapter 12, page 84

jumble mix of words that makes no sense

logical makes sense; reasonable

majority more than half the number of people counted

minority fewer than half the number of people counted

nominated named for a position that must be voted on

objects disagrees; says "no"

override to disregard what someone wants

party another word for a political group, e.g. liberal and conservative parties

policy plan or course of action, often a written plan

signature a person's name written in his or her own handwriting

specific exact; opposite of *general*

state say or write what you mean

submit send to someone

topic sentence main sentence, gives main idea of paragraph

veto say "no"

violated broke the law

Example

How the Checks and Balances System of the United States Government Protects Its Citizens

The United States system of checks and balances is designed to protect the rights of the minority as well as the majority. The three branches of government, the <u>Legislative</u> (Congress, which is composed of the members of the House of Representatives and the Senate, elected by their states), the <u>Executive</u> (the President, who is elected by the nation), and the <u>Judiciary</u> (the United States Supreme Court, whose members are nominated by the President but confirmed, or not, by the Senate) each play an important role in making and enforcing the laws.

Congress can pass (enact) a bill by a simple majority in both houses. The bill can only become a law, however, if either (1) the President signs it, or (2) after the President's veto, both houses vote to override the veto by a two-thirds majority. This protects the nation from bills designed to favor certain states, for example. Even when a bill becomes a law, either with or without the President's support, if the Supreme Court says that the law violates the United States Constitution, then the law is ruled <u>unconstitutional</u>, and is no longer a law.

The justices of the Supreme Court are another example of the checks and balances system. They are nominated by the President but must be confirmed by two-thirds of the Senate. They are appointed for life. They have the freedom to rule against popular laws if they feel that a minority's rights are being violated. With a system of checks and balances, each branch is totally dependent on the other. No one person, party, or idea has a monopoly on power. The late President Harry S Truman, when asked if he would miss being "the most powerful man on earth," said he was actually receiving a promotion as he became a citizen again, because citizens are the ones who run the country, not the President!

Used with permission of Ken Rinzler

Procedure ▼

1. Decide who or what you want to describe.

2. Using a graphic organizer (see page 84) or an outline, jot down the information you want to include.

3. Organize your information in logical or chronological (according to time) order.

4. Write your topic sentence, then use your notes to fill in your description. For example, if you are writing a description of your life, you would start from birth and work forward. If you are writing a description of a person, start either at the top or bottom and work up or down logically. The most important thing is not to jump around so the reader can't focus (can't see a clear picture).

Practice ▼

Now it's your turn.

Task: to write a descriptive paragraph

Situation: You have been asked to submit a short autobiography because you have won an award. The committee wants to know something about your background, your skills, your education, your interests. You can use the graphic organizer you made for Chapter 12.

Check your paragraph.

• Do your sentences follow logically from your topic sentence?

• Is your spelling correct?

• Did you use correct punctuation and grammar?

• Does this paragraph tell something about your background, education, skills, and interests? Save it for future use.

15 | Beginning Academic Writing

Writing a Persuasive Paragraph

We spend much of our lives trying to get people to think the same way we do. While we are busy trying to convince others, they are busy trying to convince us. Advertisers tell us why we should use their products. Politicians give us reasons to vote for them and not for their opponents. Parents tell children why they should do things as the parents say and children plot how to get their own way with their parents.

Rationale

It's important to be able to express ourselves convincingly, no matter how old we are or who we need to convince—a teacher, a parent, a child, a boss. The best way to do this is to decide what point we want to make, state it, and then give specific examples to prove it.

Materials Needed

word processor, typewriter, pen or pencil and paper, graphic organizer or outline, information or facts to prove a point

Skills Involved

organizing thoughts; focusing on a topic sentence; finding information to prove a point; writing a coherent, convincing paragraph with correct spelling, punctuation, and grammar

Important Vocabulary

add (+), subtract (−), multiply (×), divide (÷), percentage (%) terms for working with numbers

approval number a number from a credit card company saying your charge is OK

automatically done by a machine instead of by a person

change the amount of money you get back if you overpay

check out to pay before leaving a store

clerk person who takes payment at store registers

convince make someone believe something

destroying ruining; ending

endangered species something we are in danger of losing forever

opponents people on opposite sides of something

plot plan

state say or write what you mean

technology dealing with machines and science

waves passes over

Example

Modern Technology is Destroying Our Ability to Think

Modern technology is destroying our ability to think for ourselves. When we check out at the supermarket or department store, the clerk waves the items we're buying over a machine that automatically enters the price on another machine. The machine adds up the total of our purchases. The amount of money we give the clerk is entered into the machine and the machine tells the clerk how much change to give us. No one has to add or subtract, so we start to lose simple math skills before we even fully develop them. If we use a credit card, the machine prints out all the information and gets an approval number from another machine. Calculators add, subtract, multiply, divide, give percentages and do just about anything else people used to have to learn in school. Computers have programs in them that correct our spelling, so we can become lazy or careless about skills we should be improving, not losing. More and more time is spent watching television, which moves so rapidly we don't have time to think about what we're seeing. This leaves less and less time for reading, which means less time for thinking. As a result, our students are falling further and further behind those of other countries in their math and verbal skills, and thinking is becoming an endangered species.

Procedure ▼

1. Decide what point you want to make.

2. Using a graphic organizer (see page 84) or outline, jot down as many examples as you can to help you persuade others. If you need to, refer to print materials and other media for more facts. Be sure your facts are correct.

3. Organize your notes to be sure they give examples to prove your point.

4. Read over your paragraph several times, rearranging your sentences so they flow smoothly. They should stick to the topic and not jump around from one idea to another.

5. If possible, give your paragraph to someone to read. Ask for an honest response. Were you convincing?

Practice ▼

Now it's your turn.

Task: to write a persuasive paragraph

Situation: You want to convince a group that arranged marriages are far better than dating and choosing your own mate. Or, take the opposite view: dating and choosing your own mate is better than an arranged marriage. Remember to state your topic sentence and then offer specific examples, statistics (if you have any), etc., to prove your point.

Check your paragraph.

- Did you state your point clearly?

- Did you use examples to prove your point?

- Is your spelling correct?

- Did you use correct punctuation and grammar?

- Did you convince anyone?

Congratulations, even if you only convinced yourself!

Unit Five

On-the-Job Writing

16 On-the-Job Writing

Sending a Fax

"Send a fax to..." Offices all over the world have fax machines today, and many people have them in their homes. What is a fax and how do you send it? A fax is a message that is sent electronically, using a telephone line. It is sent from one fax machine to another with a special telephone number. The person sending the fax dials the receiver's fax number. When that machine answers, the message is sent and printed out through the receiver's machine. The advantage is that the fax can be sent at any hour and doesn't require anyone to be there to answer the telephone. In addition, the sender has the original copy of the message sent.

Rationale

It is not unusual to be told to fax information today, whether it's for business, to show that you have paid a bill, or to get help with a paper you are writing for school. Faxes are fast and especially good for people who are living in different time zones. If you call someone whose time zone is 14 hours earlier than yours, you know the problem. With a fax, you send it at your convenience and the receiver can read it when it's convenient at that end. No one's sleep is disturbed. No one has to be there to receive it, so long as the fax machine is on, and no immediate conversation is necessary. This makes faxes especially good for business. Knowing how to send one is an essential skill to have, even for your first job.

Materials Needed

fax machine connected to telephone line, fax telephone number for receiver, your fax number, computer or typewriter to write legible message, cover sheet, stationery (if more than one page needed), necessary information for fax

Skills Involved

operating fax machine; typing; spelling, punctuation, and grammar necessary for sending coherent message

Important Vocabulary

ASAP as soon as possible. Often used in messages.

coherent easy to understand

contact person the person to speak to in any situation

contract a written agreement between two parties telling what each is responsible for and anything else involved in the relationship

convenience at a time that is good for people

cover sheet the first page of a fax message; it gives important information

disturbed bothered, annoyed, interrupted

essential necessary

electronic works through electricity

legible it's easy to read

receiver the person to whom a message is sent

stationery unlined paper used for writing letters or sending typewritten messages

Example

FAX

Date ___July 31, 19—___

Number of pages including cover sheet ___1___

To: From:

Sandra Briggs, English Dept.   Brett Selinger

31 Fourth St.   5660 Manhattan Ave.

San Francisco, CA 93333   Fargo, North Dakota 00111

Phone: ___415 321 7654___   Phone: ___312 654 3210___

Fax Phone: ___415 321 7654___   Fax Phone: ___312 456 0593___

Message

Dear Ms. Briggs,

Mr. David Cameron, principal of our senior high school, would like you to speak to a group of local educators who are planning to visit San Francisco the week of September 10–17. They would like to know more about English programs for non-native English speakers in the San Francisco school system. They would also like to visit some programs and be able to talk to teachers and students. Would it be possible for you to arrange school meetings for 10 people, all of whom will be staying in downtown San Francisco? Please let me know dates, times, and addresses of schools to be visited and the contact person in each place. Thank you for your help.

Procedure ▼

Be sure you have the fax number of the person you are contacting, plus a cover sheet and any extra stationery you may need. If you don't have a typewriter or a computer, you can handwrite your message, but be sure to use a very dark pen so it will be legible on the other person's fax.

1. Write a practice message first so you can see how much space it will take. Try to keep your information to one page, if possible.

2. Be sure to type/write all the important information: the date, name and fax number of the person/company you're writing to, and the number of pages you're sending.

Fax Cover Sheet

Date: July 31, 19—
Number of pages including cover sheet _____

To: Ms. Electra Tonic
        Music and Poetry, Etc.

Phone: 789 987-4564
Fax Phone: 789 987-4563

---

3. Type/write your name or the name of the person the fax is from and your fax and phone numbers.

From: Neida Nightlife   *Neida Nightlife*
        Music Publishers, Inc.

Phone: 342 444-6789
Fax Phone: 342 444-6689

---

4. Type/write your message in the message box. Check your spelling, grammar, and punctuation to be sure the message is clear. Did you include all the important information?

Message

Dear Ms. Tonic,
We have decided to publish your songs "I've Gotta Learn the Language" and "That English Spelling's Killing Me" in our new book of music for English language learners. Please contact us as soon as possible so we can discuss a contract. Our office hours are Monday through Friday 8AM–4PM and Saturdays 9AM–1PM. Look forward to hearing from you ASAP as we hope to begin printing shortly.

5. Sign your name next to your printed name.

Practice ▼

Now it's your turn.

Task: to write and send a fax

Situation: Friends are coming to visit you from the town where you used to live. You want to be sure they have the right information: your address, how to get there from the train or bus station, airport, or by car, however they're planning to travel. You also want to be sure of the day and time they're coming. Send them a fax giving them the information they will need to get to your home and asking them for any information you will need, such as when they expect to arrive, how long they will be staying, etc.

FAX

Date _____
Number of pages including cover sheet _____
To: From:

_____   _____

_____   _____

_____   _____

Phone: _____   Phone: _____
Fax Phone: _____   Fax Phone: _____

<u>Message</u>

17

Writing an E-mail Letter

Congratulations. You have access to e-mail. What will you do with all the time and money you save? E-mail is so much faster and cheaper than snail mail (the term e-mailers use to talk about mail that gets addressed, stamped, and sent through the postal system). E-mail is also less expensive—you don't have to buy postage stamps, stationery, or envelopes. It is certainly the mail of the 21st century.

Rationale

E-mail (electronic mail) is a wonderful way to keep in touch with family, friends, pen pals, and the electronic world in general. You can also write letters to the editors of newspapers, order items, and correspond with people of like interests. If you have e-mail, you know your message can be sent and received immediately, and a reply can come back to you within minutes instead of days or weeks. Naturally, the person(s) you're writing to must also have an e-mail address. Many applications that ask for an address, phone number, and fax number, also ask for an e-mail address.

Materials Needed

computer, connection to one of the e-mail on-line services, e-mail screen name, address, password, e-mail address of person you are writing to

Skills Involved

signing on to e-mail; organizing thoughts; spelling, grammar, and punctuation

Important Vocabulary

access to be able use something

command order that tells the computer what to do

congratulations a way of saying you're happy for someone's good luck

correspond write to

e-mail electronic mail sent through computers

keep in touch correspond with someone so you keep connected even if you're far apart

on-line connected to an electronic service that charges by the month for use of its services

password your own secret identity code that no one else knows so only you can access your personal e-mail; many people choose their mother's maiden name (surname before she was married) or a special name they have for themselves.

pen pal a person with whom you correspond

screen name your electronic mail address that will appear on all your e-mail letters

sign on when you use e-mail, you must first type in your password, then hit the enter key to sign on

snail mail e-mailers' term for mail put in envelopes, stamped, and sent through the postal service

stationery unlined paper used for writing letters

Example

To: Natasha@BEMINSK.BE   CC:

Subject: Visit to Minsk

File:

Dear Natasha,

I miss my friends from Belarus so much! The flight home was very crowded, but smooth. It is very hot here now. School begins next week. I can't wait to tell my students about Belarus. I am sure they will want to be pen pals with your students. Please send me e-mail and snail mail addresses for your students who want pen pals here. My e-mail address is BestBev@alo.sch. Love to your family. Bev

Procedure ▼

To use e-mail the least expensive way, be sure to write your letters "off-line," not while you are paying to be on-line. Then you can press the button that says "send mail later." When you are on-line, your mail will be sent when you press the right command.

1. Type the correct e-mail address of the person where it says To:

    > To: Natasha@BEMINSK.BE

2. If you want someone else to receive a copy of the letter, type his/her e-mail address where it says CC:. Otherwise, leave that space blank.

3. In the Subject box, type a few words to tell what the letter is about.

    > Subject: Visit to Minsk

4. In the File section, type your letter. If this is the first time you're writing, be sure to include your e-mail address, even though it will show at the beginning of the letter you send. E-mail always shows who the letter is from.

5. Before sending your letter, read it again to be sure the address is correct and you have included all the information in your best English spelling and grammar.

Practice ▼

Now it's your turn.

Task: to e-mail your friend at Bestfriend@net.oal.com

Situation: You are planning a trip to visit your pen pal. You need to let your friend know when and where you are arriving and how long you will be staying. You also need to know what kind of clothes to bring for the weather there and if there is anything special they would like you to bring with you.

To:		CC:	

Subject:

File:

Check your e-mail.

- Did you write/type your friend's address correctly?

- Did you write something in the Subject box?

- Did you check your spelling, punctuation, and grammar?

- Did you include your e-mail address?

You are ready to send your e-mail!